God's Gift
of
Healing

God's Gift of Healing

by

Fred Smith

with Hilary Saunders

New Wine Press

New Wine Press
P.O.Box 17
Chichester PO20 6YB
England

ISBN 0 947852 13 1

Printed and bound in Great Britain by
Cox & Wyman Ltd, Reading

Dedication

In memory of my beloved grandaughter
Nicola

Contents

Foreword

This is a remarkable book for a variety of reasons.

First, because it is written by a retired police sergeant who discovered, to his utter amazement, that God has given him a gift of healing.

Second, because Fred knows nothing about medicine and little about theology. He has written a very practical, modest, artless account of the way God can and does do remarkable miracles of healing today in response to prayer and faith.

Third, because Fred is not in the least interested in drawing attention to himself. He sees himself as just a channel through whom God is pleased to act.

Finally, I find this book remarkable because I know and honour the man. And Fred Smith on paper is just the same as Fred Smith in the flesh — warm, friendly, sensible, humble, and full of faith in a great God who loves to answer prayer. There is no self-aggrandisement in Fred - he lives very simply, continues to be amazed that God can use him, and never receives any money for the thousands of cures in which he is instrumental.

I am delighted to write this commendation for Fred's book. His ministry is enormously appreciated in Oxford, and far beyond. Curiously enough for a non-denominational Pentecostal, most of his ministry is carried out in Anglican Churches — but he ministers only where he is asked and currently Anglicans are foremost in asking him. He has no special techniques — prayer, faith and laying on of hands suffice. Unlike anyone else I know, he takes Acts 19.11,12 as his guide and prays over cloths which are given or sent to those who wish, and are frequently used to heal. When healing is not given or retained, Fred's controversial conviction is that lack of faith or some other human obstacle, such as resentment or jealousy or unconfessed sin, may be the cause. Healing is always, he believes, God's will for men.

May God use this book to enlarge vision and increase faith. There are, St. Paul asserts, varieties of healing gifts (1 Cor. 12.9). The medical profession is one which Fred honours: the people of God at prayer is another. And a third is the particular individual gifted by God. Fred is such a man, and I, with thousands more, thank God for raising him up and keeping him humble.

Michael Green

Introduction

The telephone rang one afternoon in January 1986.

"Is that Hilary Saunders? My name is Fred Smith, and I am trying to write a book. I wondered if you would be able to help me?"

We arranged to meet, and a couple of days later Fred arrived at my door. In his arms was a large box, which I later discovered was full of letters and press cuttings about people who had been healed through his ministry.

Fred is a warm and genuine man. He told me at the beginning that he was concerned about having a book written about his ministry. "I don't want people to put me on a pedestal," he told me. "I am just the plumber's mate! It is God who does the healings — not me."

I spent the following weekend reading through the letters and press-cuttings that Fred had given me. They were an astonishing assortment, some clear and concise, others rambling and almost illegible, some only written a few weeks previously while others were dated up to twenty years ago. In their entirety they were a collection of stories which gave testimony again and again to the remarkable gift of healing which God has given to Fred.

I had never heard of Fred Smith, or of his healing ministry, until he contacted me to ask me to write this book. Some years ago I read with amazement Katherine Kuhlman's stories of her healing ministry, and for the first time I began to realise that God is still healing people in the world today. My thoughts about, and involvement with praying for the sick have been strongly influenced by the late David Watson, whose Personal Assistant I was in the eighteen months preceeding his death from cancer in 1984. During that time I had become increasingly convinced about God's healing power for today, (as had both David and his wife Anne through their contacts with John Wimber), and David's death did not diminish this conviction at all. However, I had become somewhat wary of unthinking faith healers who claimed healing when there was no healing, and the insensitive way in which Christians can sometimes treat those who are wanting ministry for healing or other problems.

Writing this book with Fred has convinced me that he is genuinely concerned for all those for whom he prays, and that he is determined to give all the glory back to God for the healings that take place. Fred makes no claim to be a theologian, but he has spent many long hours studying his Bible, and it is his interpretation of biblical teaching on healing that I have tried to reproduce. "I am a simple man, and I have a simple faith," he told me. While there may be those who are frustrated by some of his 'theology' we can rejoice in the fact that this child-like faith enables God to work through Fred so powerfully. I realise that, as in all stories of God working through human beings, it is difficult to keep a balance between what God has done, and Fred as a person. Inevitably Fred has a central part in the book, since the stories are told through his eyes, but if you feel that it is "too much Fred, and not enough Jesus" then I have failed to keep this balance, and I apologise. Both Fred and I desire that in telling this story we should give glory to God and encourage other people by telling some of the great things God has done.

Some of the stories are, for me, even now almost unbelievable! They are quite beyond the bounds of normal reason or explanation, but as I have heard the stories from Fred, or from the people who were themselves healed, I have come to realise that where God is concerned, the unbelievable becomes the believable. The major problem has been to decide which stories to include. I read the early chapters out aloud to my flatmate, Linda Smith, a sometime theologian, and while we had many questions left unanswered by Fred's stories of healing, we had also to ask why so few parts of the church in this country experience God working in this way. I am very grateful for all Linda's support and encouragment throughout the time of writing.

My parents and brothers have listened to me, encouraged me and helped me on my way; in particular I am grateful for my mother's careful and patient correction of my typing and spelling errors. Dr David Stone kindly helped me with the medical terminology, and Ruth Mounstephen patiently supported me as I struggled to finish the book. My thanks are due to them all.

I am very grateful to all those who have told their stories to us, either personally or by letter written to Fred telling of their healing. While we have made every effort to tell stories accurately, Fred has seen so many miracles, that sometimes the details may be a little vague. We apologise to any who recognise their story in this book, whose own impressions do not exactly accord with what Fred has remembered.

Fred's and my prayer is that this book will encourage the faith of many people to look to God for healing in their situation. This is not a book about the theology of healing, but about God's gift of healing in his world.

13

Today is the acceptable year of the Lord's favour — let us look to Him in faith for Him to establish what He wants for our lives.

Hilary Saunders

Oxford, July 1986

1

Crippled Joan

I turned the corner and drove along the estate. The houses were all large, with well kept gardens and pretty patterned curtains at the windows. It was a typical surburban area. But as I turned the next corner a very un-typical sight greeted me. Parked along the side of the street were four or five ambulances. I knew I had come to the right place.

It was the spring of 1976, and a few weeks earlier I had been invited to speak at a healing service in Luton. The church had been fairly crowded, and at the end of the service a large number of people had stayed to ask me to pray for their healing. Just when I thought I had come to the end the minister of the church came over to me.

"Would you be willing to come and pray for another lady, Fred?" he asked me. Well, I am always willing to pray for those who are sick and so I indicated that I was more than happy to do so. But when I looked around the church I could not see any sign of anyone waiting for me. There were still a lot of people in the church, all talking together, in small groups; people excitedly telling each other about the ways that God had been healing them that night. But there was no sign of anyone waiting for prayer at the front of the church. The minister must have seen me looking, and he answered my unspoken question. ''There's a lady waiting for us in the vestry,'' he said. ''She suffers from terrible crippling arthritis, and she is too self-conscious to ask for prayer out here in the church in front of everyone. I hope you do not mind coming into the vestry to pray.''

The minister led me into a small room just off the main part of the church, where he usually got ready for the services; there were a few books scattered on a desk and a couple of chairs. Seated on one of these chairs was one of the most severely crippled people I had ever seen. Although only middle-aged this lady looked much older as she was bent over by the effects of the arthritis. It seemed to cause her pain even to turn to look up at me as I came into the room with the minister.

As I bent down and started to talk to her, she told me that her name was Joan, and that she had suffered from the arthritis for many years. I asked her if she wanted me to pray for her, and I told her that I believed that God was able to heal her. We agreed together that I should pray, and with the minister beside me I laid hands on Joan and prayed a simple prayer, asking God to heal her, just as Jesus healed the people in the Bible, and has continued to heal down through the centuries.

Almost before I finished praying something started to happen. Her bones started to creak and crack - it sounded like the pop of a child's cap gun. Under my hands I could feel her bones straightening out, and I gently encouraged Joan to stretch her hands, then her

16

arms and legs. There was the most beautiful look on her face, as if she could hardly believe what was happening. Soon Joan was standing, straight and tall, and free from all pain. With hardly a word to me or to the minister she grasped the door handle and opening it walked out into the church.

"Look at Crippled Joan now!" she cried. As I followed her out into the church I watched her running and leaping and shouting for joy. "Look at Crippled Joan now!" The minister explained to me that this was how Joan had been known in the church, being so severely crippled. There was certainly no sign of the crippling effects of the arthritis now as she danced round the church. Joan reminded me of the story in the Bible of the lame man at the Beautiful Gate who was healed and went round the Temple 'walking and jumping and praising God' (Acts 3:1-10). It was just like that.

A few weeks later I received a phone call at my home in Abingdon. "Is that Fred Smith? This is Joan Thompson. We met a few weeks ago when you were in Luton." I had met quite a number of people on that trip so I was not sure who this lady was on the telephone. I must have sounded very uncertain. "You must remember me; I was Crippled Joan!" she laughed.

I certainly did remember her then, and at once asked how she was feeling. Joan told me that she was completely free from the pain and other debilitating effects of the arthritis, and that her doctors were amazed by her recovery. "I want to know when you are coming back to this area." she said. I explained that I only visited places when I had been invited to speak at a church service or meeting, and that at present I did not have any plans to visit her area again. Joan sounded very disappointed, but then her voice perked up. "Do you only go to church meetings?" she asked, "Or would you be prepared to come to my house one day?"

Joan explained that she had been attending a clinic for the chronically crippled and disabled. Her next appointment had been about ten days after I had prayed with her, and she had gone to the clinic to show everyone what had happened to her. She described the scene as she walked into the clinic, tall and straight, wearing high heeled shoes, which she had not been able to do for some time. Initially people could hardly believe that it was really Joan, and when she told them how God had healed her they were astonished. Several other chronically crippled people had scribbled down their names and addresses, and had asked Joan to let them know when I was next coming to Luton so that they could come for prayer as well.

Joan explained her idea to me. "If you have not been invited to come back to the church in the immediate future, would you consider coming to meet these people in my house? I could invite them all to tea, and then you could talk to them about Jesus and pray with them." I was very moved by the description of the other crippled folk at the clinic, so we settled on a date for me to go to her house to meet these people. "But you must remember Fred, that they are chronically disabled," she warned me.

It seemed no time at all until I was on my way to her house. I could guess at once which was Joan's house. No other house had several ambulances parked outside the door having brought those who were least mobile. Just after I arrived I watched another group of people arriving at Joan's house. A lady with irons on both legs was moving slowly towards the house. A couple walked one on either side of her, with their arms around her shoulders supporting her. The woman was balancing her weight on two walking sticks, and as the man at her side pushed one foot forward she reached forward with one stick, then the other as the woman on her other side pushed the other foot towards the stick. The little group made tortuously slow progress, and my heart went out to the woman. Obviously Joan had not exaggerated the extent of her friends' disabilities.

After Joan had greeted me and given me a cup of tea she ushered me into her sitting room. It was a good sized room, pleasantly decorated, but today it looked very overcrowded. There must have been about eighteen people seated round the room, many so obviously crippled that it was easy to understand the presence of so many ambulances in the road outside.

As I looked round the room, seeing a mixture of hope and fear, pain and tiredness etched on so many of the faces it was impossible not to feel a deep compassion for each person there. How many of them would receive healing that afternoon? It is at times like this that I am so glad that it isn't anything about me that gets people healed. All I can ever do for people is to pray and ask God to do his healing work. Sometimes it feels rather as though I am the plumber's mate, and God is the plumber. My job is to stand in the right place, and hand him the tools he requires so that he can do what needs to be done, the tools being my hands and prayers. All healing is the work of God Almighty, and we should be continually praising and thanking Him for such great love and compassion towards children who continue to rebel and reject Him.

Like the plumber's mate who has confidence in his boss, so I have confidence in God's skill to do the job. The responsibility for healing lies with God, not me. Of course that does not mean that I am not very concerned to see people healed. I have been praying for people for over twenty-five years now, and I have seen

God doing marvellous healings. This gathering of people at Crippled Joan's house certainly needed God's healing power.

I introduced myself to the group, and looking round at them all I commented that I did not think I had previously met any of them. A young woman sitting on the floor in front of the fireplace smilingly interrupted me. ''You have met me before.'' she said. ''I had cancer a few years ago and you prayed for me and God healed me. But now they tell me that I cannot have children. My husband and I desperately want a baby so I thought that if I came today you might pray for me again.

So of course I prayed for her. It was a great encouragement for me to hear her story, and I was glad too that she had told everyone in the room. Firstly they had seen how God had healed Joan. Now here was someone else, healed from a terminal illness. These two very different stories might encourage the others there that God could do something for them. (A couple of years later a woman came up to speak to me after a service carrying a beautiful girl. She asked me if I remembered praying for a child for her, and told me that it had been this occasion at 'Crippled' Joan's house. ''This is the little girl that God gave me,'' she said, ''in answer to our prayers.'')

I did not know anything about the other people in the room, so after I prayed for the girl I spent some time talking to them all. I told them that I believed that God loves us and wants us to know and love Him, that I do not believe that sickness is ever part of God's plan for our lives, and that He is longing to heal us. I talked about some of the people that Jesus healed in the Bible, and then I told some stories about people today whom I had seen healed in answer to prayer. I wanted to encourage them to believe that God is a healing God, so that they might start to expect Him to do something for them.

As I finished speaking I looked round the room, and I felt the Lord prompting me to pray for the woman I had seen arriving at the house with irons on both her legs. I talked to her briefly to discover the extent of her disability, and then I prayed a short simple prayer. I was confident that God was healing her, and in her eyes I could see that she felt the same thing. I took her hands, and spoke gently. "You told me that you expected to be healed, so now I want you to stand up, in the name of Jesus." She started to stand, then of her own accord she bent down and started to undo the straps which held her leg irons in place. "I am sure that without these irons on I will be able to bend my legs" she said. And she was right. She was able to stand unaided, and had no difficulty bending her knees and lifting her legs. Soon she was raising her knees quite high, like a soldier marking time. Her face was radiant. Sometimes encouraging people to do something to find out what has happened, like reaching out or standing up in faith will seal their healing as they demonstrate their faith, especially on occasions like this when, through the spiritual gift of knowledge from the Holy Spirit, I know that they are indeed healed. Within a few minutes she had taken my hands and we were dancing

"Knees up Mother Brown" on the carpet in the middle of the floor. It was clear that she had been dramatically and miraculously healed.

I left the lady to celebrate and turned to start praying for the next person. But the man whom I had seen escorting the lady to the house came over to me, demanding to speak to me outside. I tried to persuade him to wait until I had finished praying, but he became quite agitated and I realised that he could not wait to talk to me.

As soon as we got outside the door into the small hallway his story came out. "I am an ordained minister", he burst out, telling me that he had come to see what I was doing, and that in order to prevent me knowing who he was he had purposefully worn an ordinary tie instead of a clerical collar. He asked me to pray with him, asking God to forgive him. "I did not believe that God heals today, so when I heard about this meeting I brought along the most severely crippled member of my church, just to prove my point." Instead, God seemed to have proved his point when he healed the woman so dramatically.

Back in the sitting-room I started to pray for each person in turn. Having seen the first crippled lady healed so completely and miraculously many of them were convinced that they too would receive their healing, and they came to a new faith in God. In all the excitement I cannot remember exactly what happened to each person, but we saw the vast majority of those chronically crippled people completely healed. Of all those who had arrived so badly crippled in ambulances only two or three had to leave in the ambulance, and of those not completely healed some could see a marked improvement in their mobility. It was an amazing sight watching the empty ambulances leave, and we praised God for all that He had done that afternoon.

As I drove quietly away some time later my heart was full of joy at all that had happened. There were still some questions that I could not answer. Why had God not healed everyone? Why did God choose to work through me, a retired policeman, with the most ordinary name imaginable, Fred Smith?

2

The Growing Up Years

My earliest memories are of hearing the news of the end of the First World War, announced over loud hailers in the city of Worcester. My mother hurried me along the road to tell my grandparents the news, much faster than my short four-year-old legs — and my sense of dignity — thought I should go.

My father worked for the Great Western Railway, and both my brother — two years my senior — and I were born in Worcester. Our sister Muriel, several years younger than I, was the baby of the family. We two boys were about as different as two brothers can be. Ron was a rather delicate, quiet, well-behaved lad, while I was always getting up to mischief, and getting caught. My father, who was a strict and solemn man would beat me regularly, but he could never crush my sense of fun and mischief.

One of my most successful pranks was when I persuaded my brother to join me knocking the last remaining apple off the top of our garden tree. We tried shaking the branches to dislodge the apple; next we tried to hit the apple with all kinds of missiles until finally it came down. Success! From our vantage point in the garden we watched Dad's mother leaving our house, getting onto her oldfashioned bicycle to ride up the road. Grandma Smith was a dour Victorian matriarch, probably even less fond of children than her son, and her visits caused us real misery when she criticised us and complained about everything we did. The apple offered us the perfect chance for revenge. My brother offered me the shining red apple: "I bet you could not hit Grandma with this apple." I took aim, stepped back and let go. It was a perfect hit! But our hilarity turned to panic when Dad turned in at the gate at just that moment to find his mother lying sprawled in a sea of black petticoats with her shopping scattered about her. It did not take Dad long to track down the culprits, nor to identify me as the one with the bright ideas, and since he thought that Ron was too delicate to be beaten, on this particular occasion I think I got his share of the punishment as well as my own.

We belonged to the Baptist Chapel in Worcester, and attended services regularly Sunday by Sunday. Early each Sunday morning my brother and I were collected by a 'big girl', who must have been all of nine or ten, and she would escort us to Sunday school. After that came the morning service, and usually we went back again in the evening. It seemed as though it was the number of times you went to chapel that counted with God, even though I understood very little of what I heard. It all seemed quite irrelevant to me. The elderly minister was a kind, friendly man, but his sermons were long and very complex. I remember overhearing a man talking to my father as we left the chapel after one morning service. "I thought Jesus said 'feed the sheep'" he commented. "You would have to be a giraffe to reach anything from this minister.''

My mother used to sing in the chapel choir at the evening service, which meant she could not sit with us to control us. The choir sat in a gallery at the front of the church above the pulpit area, and since Dad did not have to look after us, Ron and I were seated up in another gallery at right angles to where Mother was sitting. Since we were usually the only two up in the gallery it was easy for her to keep an eye on us during the service, and we had a marvellous time looking down on everyone else. What we did not realise was that our high level vantage point meant that we were clearly visible to everyone else. On one occasion when I was about five years old a loose front tooth came out during the sermon. I managed to signal to my mother, and pointed out the gap in my mouth to show what had happened. Then I put the tooth on the rail in front of me, and indicated that I was going to flick it over to her so that she could inspect it, and share my excitement. Mother tried her best to stop me, shaking her head violently, and frowning at me, but I ignored her warning. I balanced the tooth carefully on the rail, took aim and flicked it as hard as I could. It sailed across the church towards the choir, but my aim was not quite accurate enough. The tooth fell short, and landed smack in the middle of the minister's Bible as he stood preaching at the pulpit. What a hit! Little did I realise that I had managed to attract the attention of everyone in the congregation by this time, and completely destroyed the effect of the sermon.

Family life was not easy with my father, so it came as a pleasant relief when he was promoted to a job which took him away from home for several days at a time. It also meant a move for the whole family to the town of Malvern, and it was in these beautiful surroundings that I spent most of my growing-up years. There were plenty of wide open spaces where children could play, and I spent many happy hours exploring and inventing wild games to play with my friends.

The move also meant transfering from the chapel at Worcester to one at Malvern, but it made little difference to me. If anything, the services meant even less to me now. But I was soon to become completely disillusioned with religion. My uncle came to visit us, and as a belated birthday present he pressed a two-shilling coin into my hand when he left. Two shillings! This was wealth beyond my wildest dreams. I spent several happy hours planning all the things I could buy. First stop was the sweet shop. In the window were rows of large glass jars full of brightly coloured sweets, wrapped in twists of paper, the sort you could have by the pennyworth. I spent a long time with my nose pressed hard against the glass making my selection. If I had a pennyworth of these striped ones, then a pennyworth of raspberry ones I would hardly have dented my two-shillings at all. With my mind made up I opened the shop door and went inside. I knew the shopkeeper quite well, since he was one of the men who greeted us at the door at chapel each Sunday, handing out the hymnbooks. He smiled warmly as I held up my precious coin and asked for the sweets. Soon I was holding two little paper bags, and I held out my hand for the change. First a sixpence, then four coppers. I looked down at my hand in dismay — that was only change for one shilling.

"Excuse me, but that's not right" I blurted out. "I gave you a two shilling piece!"

"Now don't you try that on me" the man replied, "you know it was only a shilling."

"But that is my two-shilling piece on the counter"

I pointed out.

"Enough of your nonsense; that was left by the previous customer" he said. And with that he swept the coin up into his till.

I glared at him in disbelief. He knew, and I knew that it was my two-shillings. I was so angry I could feel the tears smarting in my eyes. I knew my parents would never believe me if I told them that I had been cheated. After all, the man was a sidesman at church, and I was only a grubby kid. What a hypocrite! I turned and walked out of the shop furious and frustrated. All my dreams shattered, and only tenpence left. All the years of going to chapel every week, and now I discovered that it was all fake — this man had his smile of welcome on Sunday, but he was only too keen to steal from a child. "That does it" I said to my brother. "I don't want anything to do with these hypocrites and their religion. As soon as I am old enough to choose, I am never going to go back to chapel!" And that was it — as soon as my parents gave me the choice I was never to be seen inside the chapel again.

When my brother left school he got a job working for a company bottling Malvern water. There is a natural mineral water spring in the hills around the town, which had been awarded prizes for the purest water in the world. Malvern was a Victorian spa, and the area around the spring was known as St Ann's Well. The town of Malvern had grown up around the spa, with rows of houses built on the hills. It is a beautiful town, nestling on the side of the hills. On the west side of the range is a famous beauty spot, Jubilee Drive, where Queen Victoria had driven on a visit to the town in her Jubilee year. The spa was a great tourist attraction, providing mineral water for all who came to drink, but most of the water was bottled and marketed down in the town by the company for whom my brother worked. People from all over the country would place regular orders for a crate of bottles at a time. Ron worked in the accounts department as a clerk, and was so conscientious and hard working that he was quickly promoted, and he obviously enjoyed it very much.

I was so jealous of him as I set off for school each morning. My parents had given an undertaking to Worcester Royal Grammer School that I would stay on until seventeen, but I was not a keen student, and I longed to leave school as soon as possible. When I was nearly 16 my brother was offered a better job with the Local Authority, so he handed in his notice. I could see that this was my chance. I knew that my brother had been conscientious and hard-working and hoped that the company might like to employ his brother in his stead. I did not tell anyone of my plans, but the following afternoon I left home as normal after lunch, but instead of heading back to school I set off up the hill out of Malvern to the factory.

I waited for a while and was then called in to talk to the manager. I told him that since my brother was leaving the company I wondered whether I could have his job instead. I suppose it was rather presumptuous, but I was desperate to get out of school, and I hoped that Ron's good reputation might get me a job. We talked for a while, and the manager asked me all manner of questions. ''Does your father know you are here?'' he asked me. I had to admit that I had come for an interview without telling anyone of my plans. Malvern was only a small town, and the manager knew my father, and probably knew something of his strict discipline. He laughed, and agreed to give me the job. I was so excited I could hardly get out of his office without whooping with delight. No more school, and ten shillings each week. Life was looking up!

There was still the problem of what I was going to tell Dad. I had won a scholarship for a covetted place at Worcester Royal Grammar School, but there were certain conditions attached to the scholarship. My parents had to agree that I would stay on for the sixth-form. Now that I was going to leave early they would have to pay the school fees for the time I failed to complete. There was quite a scene that night when I told my parents and for a while I thought Dad would have apoplexy as he got so worked up. But he finally agreed to let me leave school, on the understanding that I gave him my wages each week to pay back the forfeited school fees, and he would give me a small sum for myself. It was quite a price to pay, but it was worth it.

Perhaps it was not the most exciting job in the world, but for me it was perfect. I spent many happy hours making out invoices in my best copper-plate hand-writing. Fifty years later I can still remember some of the regular customers. There was a doctor in the Midlands who ordered so much water I could only think he used to bathe his children in it, and another regular order went to New Zealand. I can still remember some of the addresses for the regular invoices. It could have been rather a boring environment for an active young man, but there was plenty going on in the office. Although I was growing up fast I had yet to learn to distinguish between a joke and when my jokes went too far.

As the most junior member of the department it was my job to answer the door when people came to visit my boss. On one occasion my sense of humour over-came me. As I showed the visitor into the boss's office I warned him ''You will have to shout; he is quite deaf, but he does not like people to know.'' ''Good morning!'' the man duly shouted as he walked into the office. In fact there was nothing wrong with the boss's hearing, but when this man started to shout he assumed that his visitor was hard of hearing, so answered in a loud voice. I stood outside the door rocking with laughter at the sound of these two businessmen shouting at each other.

At last they stopped shouting. Both discovered that the other was not in fact hard of hearing, and it was not long before my boss realised that I was the culprit. I was called in to see him, and he told me that the question of my continuing employment was under review, and that he would tell me his decision at the end of the week. It was a terrible few days, as I worried about how I could tell my father if I lost my job. On the Friday morning the Chief Cashier sent me to the bank to collect the wages, and on the way back to the office I stopped at a public telephone box. I dialled the number of my company, and trying to disguise my voice I asked the girl on the switchboard whether there was a vacancy for a junior clerk, either now or in the near future. After a brief pause the girl returned to the telephone. ''I have asked the manager, and he does not anticipate any such a vacancy in the foreseeable future,'' she told me. I tried to sound disappointed as I said goodbye, but it was the best news I could have heard. If there was no vacancy it meant that I still had a job. I returned to work feeling as though I was walking on air, and it was not until many years later that I admitted to my boss quite how nervous I had been on that occasion.

Although I enjoyed my job in the accounts department it was not the sort of job I wanted to spend my life in. After four years with the company I started to look around for a new career, particularly wanting a job which would enable me to afford to get married. I had started courting a local girl, Stella, and it was not long before I felt sure that I wanted to marry this beautiful girl. Luckily she felt that she would like to marry me, and I wanted to settle down into a job with suitable prospects. Shortly after I was 20 I joined the Royal Berkshire Constabulary, and went to work at the Police Headquarters in Reading. This meant that at long last I could leave home. I had been longing for a reason to leave home for some time, as my father was still taking most of my wages and keeping strict control on everything I did. Life in the police force, with all its discipline, would be a welcome relief.

3

Life with the Police

Stella and I continued courting throughout my first couple of years with the force. The police training was demanding but enjoyable, and I soon made many good friends. After a while I was transferred to the Traffic Department and became a motor-cycle outrider, a speed cop. Sometimes I was attached to the royal family on their Windsor visits, and it was on a trip to Ascot Races that I had a serious accident. I had been detailed to escort the late Duke of Connaught's car to Ascot Races, and I was on my way to collect him from Windsor Castle and had reached the village of Binfield when a milk lorry swerved across the road and hit me head on. I remember the lorry bearing down on me, and knowing there was no way that a crash could be avoided I can remember looking up for a last look at the sky. Then I was flung off the bike and landed several yards away on a heap of gravel. I landed on my back and, as my eyes registered on the sky above my first thought was that I was dead. Then I realised that my right arm was smashed so badly that it was twisted behind me with my hand resting on my shoulder from behind me. They later found two pieces of bone several inches long jammed in the milk lorry's radiator.

A passing painter and decorator in a van offered to take me to hospital. I can still remember the smell of the paint pots lying round me in the back of the van, as I asked the driver to take me to the police station. As soon as the doctor had inspected me and seen the extent of my injuries I was rushed to the Royal Berkshire hospital. The first of many operations lasted over five hours, but the surgeons were able to save my arm. I was on the sick list for nearly two years, and spent much of that time in and out of hospital. I had to have 12 major operations, with a series of bone grafts to replace the bone which had splintered. I was let out of hospital in between the operations, and to begin with I went to stay with my parents so that they could look after me. It was very difficult to manage on my own when I could only use my left hand. Then my father was posted to a different part of the country by his employer, and my parents moved away from the district while I was still under the care of the Reading hospital. I did not know how I would cope without them.

I was sent to see the Deputy Chief Constable, and I explained the situation to him. "You are courting, aren't you?" he asked me. When Stella and I had decided to get married I had notified our intention to the force, because police officers were not allowed to marry without permission in those days, and anyway no one was allowed to marry until he had been in the force for four years as a single man. The Deputy Chief Constable agreed to waive the four year rule in my case, and suggested that if Stella was still willing to marry me we should bring forward the date of the wedding so that she could look after me until I was fully fit again.

To my great relief and joy Stella agreed to this plan, and we started to plan the wedding. I still needed more hospital care, and it was not the easiest way to start married life, but Stella was marvellous at caring for me, as she has been ever since. When Stella and I got married in December 1937 in Malvern it was the first time I had been to a service since my parents had given me the choice. It was also the last service I attended for several years.

When I was declared fit again I went back to work, glad to put the accident firmly behind me. Soon after that I joined CID, and enjoyed this new role very much. During the next fifteen years I worked my way up and became a sergeant and eventually station sergeant at Abingdon. It was a fairly normal police career. As part of my CID role I was attached to the judges' circuit when they came for the Assize Courts. The escort is meant to go everywhere with the judge, and that included the morning service in church to ask God's blessing on their deliberations. I did not want to go to church, because I would feel hypocritical, so I would see the judge safely inside the building, then I would go round the back of the church for a cigarette. I would watch out for the judge coming out, so that I could nip round to the car and be ready to escort him to the courts. On the whole it was an enjoyable time with CID. I made close friendships with the other men, and Stella was very kind and welcoming to them all, so our home became something of a base for off-duty single policemen.

During the Second World War all policemen under the age of 25 were called up into the armed services. I was just 25 and I missed the call-up date by a matter of months. The Police Force was classified as a reserve occupation, so I stayed with the police throughout the war, serving with CID, as we tried to keep peace at home and facilitate the war effort as best we could.

Stella and I were both keen to start a family and we were delighted with our two children, Patricia and Roger, who were both born during the war. When the children were small we used to spend most of our holidays visiting both sets of grandparents at Worcester and Malvern. Even though I was a grown man, with a wife and two children I still did not get on well with my father, and I did not look forward to these visits home. Not only was my father such a cold unloving man, but my mother seemed to have become fanatical about going to the Baptist chapel. It was enormously important to her. If we were staying with my parents for a weekend I felt I should go to chapel with my family. "Well, mother would like it!" But this was not enough to keep her quiet. As I drove towards their house I could just imagine mother starting what I called "Bible bashing". "Have you been to chapel?" "No I haven't, Mother" "Well, there is this man in our chapel who says this, or does that. You really ought to go and hear him." I knew how the conversation would go.

But on one particular visit Mother seemed far less pushy than normal about going to chapel. I soon realised why. "There is a minister of a church in Worcester who is holding some special services this week. His name is Ken Matthew, and I don't really know what he is like," Mother told me, "but they say he has a divine healing ministry. He prays for the sick and lays hands on them in the name of Jesus, and all sorts of marvellous things are happening. Crippled people are being healed and leaving their crutches behind, and blind people are able to see."

As we went to bed that night I told Stella about this

37

conversation. "Mother has really gone over the top now" I said. "She's got religious mania. These sort of things just don't happen!"

Mother went to these services each night and the next morning at breakfast she would tell us about all the things that had happened. She always encouraged us to go with her, and each day I had to think up a different excuse. When it came to Friday morning, the day of the last service, I had my excuse all prepared, and felt quite safe with it. But instead of telling us about all sorts of unbelievable miracles, Mother asked me if I remembered a blind old lady who had frightened me when I was a child in Worcester. She looked just how I imagined a witch would look, as she tapped her way around Worcester with her white stick in front of her, and her long white hair plaited down her back. "Well, she is not blind any more," Mother said. "She received her sight at the meeting last night."

I had to see this! I guess deep down inside I thought that with my CID detective training I would be able to spot what this charlatan was doing. He was obviously tricking them somehow. I knew my mother would never purposely tell lies, but I was quite sure that the stories could not be true. Stella and I would go along that evening and I would play the great detective and discover what was really going on so that I could put Mother right.

The meeting was very different from what I had expected. Ken Matthew was more like a minister leading a chapel service than the showman I had expected. He spoke quite simply, telling the Bible story of Nicodemus who came secretly to Jesus by night. Jesus told the man he needed to be born again; "We also need to be born again," explained Ken Matthew.

The phrase 'born again' did not have the same

hackneyed American political connotations it has today. This was a new idea for me. Ken talked about how God forgives us because Jesus died on the Cross, and that He gives us a new life with Him, and gives us His power in our lives. "It is through Jesus' victory over death on the Cross that we are both saved and healed; the Bible tells us that, 'By His stripes we are healed'."

At the end of his talk Ken Matthew asked anyone who wanted to put things right with God to stand up and come to the front. I could not move. My whole life seemed to have been turned upside down during the talk, all my ideas and priorities challenged, but I felt as though I was stuck to my seat by a thick layer of glue. I remember quite clearly pushing myself to my feet, only to find that I could hardly move my legs. It was as though I was wearing a pair of weighted diver's boots on my feet, making them too heavy to move.

Somehow I got out of the row of seats and started to make my way to the front. I realised somewhat to my surprise that I had tears running down my cheeks. I am not the kind of man who cries easily, and the talk I had just heard was not a case of emotional rhetoric. I suppose that the tears were expressing my own feelings about myself and repentance towards God in the light of what I had heard, and my realisation that I could start again with God. But I was embarrassed to be crying in front of so many strangers. I managed to walk down an aisle near the wall, and I kept my face turned away from all the people sitting by the aisle. Imagine me, a grown man, a police sergeant at that, crying at a religious service. I could hardly believe it myself! Ken Matthew must have seen my tears, and he took pity on me. "Don't be embarrassed by tears," he said. "There is nothing more precious to God than when we come to him so vulnerable, wanting to repent for our sins and put things right with God.''

I do not know whether there were any miraculous healings that evening. In fact I remember very little about the rest of the meeting apart from suddenly realising that God was true and important to me. The hypocrisy that I had met as a child meant nothing now. I met with God in a new way, and I realised that if God could forgive me for all my sins and for the ways I had ignored him, then he could forgive the man with the sweet shop in Malvern, and all the others who had put me off chapel. But I realised that becoming a Christian meant everything. I was not going to be a half-hearted Christian. I did not want anyone to look at my life and be put off God by me.

When our holiday was over and we came back to Newbury I was excited about the things God had shown me, and about my new faith in Him. Although I tried going to some of the local churches I found that the preaching was not like the clear simple messages about Jesus that I had heard from Ken Matthew. I did not want to listen to sermons about the slums of Liverpool as I did on one occasion in Church — in my enthusiasm for my new faith I failed to realise that God cares for each of us, and particularly for the poor and needy. As far as I was concerned it was much more exciting to see God healing people, and seeing souls saved. So for a while I started commuting all the way to Worcester every Sunday to go to Ken Matthew's church. If I was on night duty I would come home for breakfast on Sunday morning, then drive down to Worcester for the morning service. Or if I was on the early shift I could be in Worcester in time for the evening service. Although this meant a round trip of over one hundred and fifty miles each Sunday it was worth all the time and the cost of the petrol as far as I was concerned.

I was hungry to hear and see more about God, and I wanted to learn everything I could.

On my trips to Worcester I would often visit some cousins of mine who had also become Christians at one of Ken Matthew's services. They were a few weeks ahead of me, and I could see the difference that their faith had made to them, so I would spend many hours talking and praying with them. They encouraged me to read my Bible, and spend time praying to God on my own. "Listening to God" they called it. They also talked to me about receiving the power of the Holy Spirit into my life. God's gift to His children, the Holy Spirit comes into our lives when we accept Jesus, but often we need to release our lives to Him, and allow Him to work in us and through us in power. My cousins prayed for me to receive this precious empowering by the Holy Spirit of God, and I found myself falling deeper and deeper 'in love' with God.

After a while Ken Matthew noticed me in church Sunday after Sunday, and he stopped me at the door to talk to me. I suppose he assumed I had recently moved into Worcester. When I explained that I had just become a Christian, but that I lived in Newbury and came down each week for the service he was amazed. He was humble enough to realise that it was not his gift of speaking that attracted me, rather the sense of God's presence and the signs of Him at work in the Church.

Ken and I became firm friends, and he recognised that becoming a Christian had meant a radical change in my life. He was able to help me work through all the different issues associated with my new values and loyalties as a Christian. It was not easy to be a Christian policeman. From being the life and soul of the police station, I now felt as though I had lost all my friends. Whether my colleagues felt threatened by my new faith, or thought that I was less concerned about them now that I had 'got religious' I will never know. But it was a painful time as I felt more and more cut off from those around me.

Perhaps this was why I so appreciated getting away to church at Worcester each week. Worshipping God was one of the most beautiful experiences of my life. And there was always something new to learn from Ken Matthew's sermons. So I was delighted, if a little surprised, when Ken asked me to accompany him on a preaching trip he had been asked to do. I was keen to go, but a little unsure what I could do to help. Ken explained that he needed someone to help with the organisation, to be around to help when he prayed for people, and also he thought it would be a good experience for me.

I managed to arrange for a few days holiday at the right time, and went off with Ken as he suggested. They were some of the most exciting days of my life. My love for God was such that I wanted to hear more and more about Him, but more than anything I wanted others to come to know Him too. When he preached Ken always encouraged people to commit their hearts and lives to God, and night after night people would respond. When I saw people healed through the power of prayer it was just like the Bible come to life. Sometimes people would seem to fall asleep under the power of the Holy Spirit when Ken prayed. It wasn't that they fainted, rather that they were overwhelmed by the love and power of God. Sometimes Ken would ask me to be ready to catch people if they were overwhelmed in this way. Gradually he made me get more and more involved in the services. One night I had to stand on the platform to give out some notices. Another night I had to sing a solo hymn. Ken really caught me out on that occasion. He knew I enjoyed singing, but was far too shy to sing in public, so he simply announced that I was going to sing, and turning to where I was sitting on the stage behind him, he handed me the microphone and that was it. Although that particular evening was rather embarrassing the rest of the services were a real delight, and I was so excited to be involved with God's work. Everything else seemed rather less exciting in comparison.

Ken Matthew encouraged me to get involved in a fellowship near my home, rather than spend so much time travelling. He suggested one church that we could attend as a family, which we joined. I suspect that nothing could have been quite the same as the church in Worcester, or my privileged role with Ken on his preaching trip. The church we joined seemed a little less exciting, but I knew that it was the same God whom we were worshipping.

I did find it hard that I could not always go to the morning communion service. Receiving Holy Communion had become very special to me, a real symbol of my new relationship with God, reminding me that Jesus died and rose again. But my police duties meant I could only get to one service each Sunday, and that was dependent on which shift I was working. I was complaining about this to some Christian friends one day, and laughed when one of them suggested I should ask for every Sunday off. No policeman ever gets a regular day off like that, let alone a station sergeant. "Even if I asked the Chief Constable himself I would never be given every Sunday off!"

"I did not mean that you should ask your boss," replied my friend. "Why don't you ask your heavenly Father? What kind of God do you believe in, after all?"

I waited till everyone else had gone to bed, then I got down on my knees to pray. I did not even want Stella to hear this prayer. I knew it said in the Bible that 'with God all things are possible', but this seemed a hard thing to ask. But I prayed anyway, and asked God to arrange it for me to have Sundays off.

On the following Saturday afternoon the Superintendent called me into the office. I knew he wanted something from me, because he called me by my name, rather than just 'sergeant.'

"Fred, I'd like a word with you" he said. "Look, I don't like it when you are not here during the week. If you have a day off on Monday, Tuesday or Wednesday things don't run so smoothly. The quietest day of the week is Sunday and I wondered if you would do me a favour and take Sunday as your day off in future, starting tomorrow." The Lord had answered my prayer, and I did not work on a single Sunday over the next seven years until I retired. When the next Station Sergeant came to take over from me he went back to working on Sundays just like everyone else. I am the only policeman I know who had every Sunday off. Seeing God answer my prayer encouraged me to ask for other things, and God answered them too.

Going to church was even more special to me now. We had settled happily into our local church, and when we went on holiday I would look for another church to attend. For one family holiday we stayed with Stella's parents. We arrived on the Saturday, and on the Sunday morning when I was praying about the day God put a picture of a church into my mind, and it was as though I heard this voice telling me to go and preach there. It was a church we had driven past on the previous day, so I knew where it was, but I had never preached in my life, and it wasn't something I was keen to do.

I went downstairs and told Stella about this picture, and asked what she thought. "Well, it is already 10.30 on Sunday morning," she said. "Do you think they have been waiting for you to arrive on your holiday so that you can preach to them? I think you must have got it wrong."

I went back upstairs and prayed again. Again I sensed God telling me the same thing; "Go and preach in this church." So I told Stella that I thought I had better go to the church, in case it was God telling me. She decided not to come along and I was quite relieved at her decision. I did not want her to see me make a fool of myself if I did have to preach.

I found the church without too much difficulty, and went inside just as the service started. To my relief there was a minister leading the service, and he preached the sermon. When it got to the last hymn I realised that there was not any appropriate place in the service for me to speak so, rather relieved, I just closed the hymn book and prayed quietly about the whole episode. I must have misunderstood what God was saying.

I was one of the first to leave the church, but the minister was standing waiting in the porch. He had come out during the final hymn, and was ready to greet everyone as they left. As I reached him he held out his hand, and I expected him to ask if I was a visitor or something like that. "Will you preach to us tonight?" he asked. He had not even asked my name. I thought I had better agree, then slipped away as fast as I could.

"Well, did you get to preach?" asked Stella when I got in. "Not this morning, but I've got to preach tonight. Can you remember a good sermon you have heard recently?" I thought that we might be able to remember enough between us and I could use it. But we could not remember enough to last for a sermon.

I had not been a Christian for very long, and I did not know my Bible very well. There was no easy sermon tucked up my sleeve. I spent the whole afternoon looking through my Bible, waiting for inspiration to strike. By the time it was six o'clock I was no further forward. About all I could say was, "My name is Fred Smith and I am a policeman." Not exactly a powerful sermon!

When I arrived at the service there were two ministers present, and I slipped quietly into one of the pews hoping they wouldn't notice me. But after the first hymn the minister leading the service stood up. "I believe that God has sent His servant along with a message for us tonight." At this he smiled at me, and beckoned me forward. It seemed a very long way up to the pulpit, and I prayed for inspiration all the way. When I got to the pulpit and turned to face the congregation they looked like row after row of hungry chickens waiting for a message from God. "Let us pray" I said. I prayed for as long as I decently could, but I had to stop sometime. I still had no idea at all about what I should say. "Well, its up to you God!" I whispered.

Then God started to speak through me. It was my voice all right, but I was listening just like everyone else. These were not my thoughts or ideas — it was God's message to His people, all about healing relationships and healing the church. After about twenty minutes the message stopped. God had finished speaking. It is very difficult to describe what I mean, but it was as though I was just the voice and body God used. The effect was powerful. There were people crying, hugging one another, crossing the aisle to greet each other. Someone came up to me and explained that the church had been divided into two groups for over five years, that the previous minister had left because it was such an impossible situation, and that people had even refused to speak to each other if they met out in the town. Tonight God had brought peace and reconciliation. I left quietly. There was nothing else for me to do there — God had already done what He wanted.

Preaching seemed really easy. All you had to do was stand there and open your mouth. God would do the rest! At least that was what I thought. But I was quite content to sit back at my home church and let the minister do the preaching. As I stood outside the church one morning, waiting to cross the road to my car a stranger came up to me. "I saw you come out of that church didn't I?" he asked. "That's right" I replied. "Well it says on the notice board that the sick are prayed for after each service. I have been coming for six weeks, and nobody has prayed for me, and I am in deep and desperate trouble." So I apologised on behalf of the pastor and congregation. "If you come back tonight I will make sure that someone prays with you."

That was not going to satisfy him. "I can't go on any longer," he said. "The pain is too bad." He told me he was going to commit suicide. I offered to ring the Samaritan emergency line, or get him some help, but he would not have any of that. "Why don't you pray for me?" he said. "Well, I'm not a priest or minister or anything like that," I started to explain. "That doesn't matter," he said. "Don't you know how to pray? Then you pray for me to be healed."

4

Praying for the Sick

We were standing on one of the main streets in Oxford. I did not know what to do, but the man was desperate; perhaps I had better pray for him. After all, I had watched Ken Matthew and others pray for the sick. All they did was ask God to heal the person. I could ask that too.

I took the man into a shop doorway so that we were out of the noise of the passing traffic. I had watched and listened when Ken Matthew prayed for people to be healed, so I thought I had better do what I had seen him do. I asked God to anoint my hands, to use them as instruments of His healing power. When I laid my hands on the man he jerked a few inches in the air. It rather frightened me. "What's the matter?" I asked urgently. "Thank you, thank you; the pain has completely gone." he replied.

I did not know what to think. I was rather embarrassed and did not want anyone to see us. Nor would I tell anyone about it. Saying I had prayed for someone and he had been healed would be rather like telling people that I had seen a flying saucer. I thought they might try to lock me up in hospital! So I went home quickly without finding out anything more about the man, and I did not tell anyone.

Ten days later I was walking up the central shopping street of Abingdon in my police uniform on my way to meet one of the constables out on the beat. It was market day and the shopping centre was crowded with people. As I made my way through the crowds a woman came up and stopped me. "Excuse me sergeant ...." As a policeman in uniform I must have been asked every imaginable question ranging from the time of day, and directions to endless places, to complaints about everything under the sun. But I had never been asked this question before.

"Excuse me sergeant, will you pray for me?"

Well it was not quite what I was expecting. "Why did you ask me that?" I questioned her. "Well sergeant, it is rather difficult to explain, but I am a Christian and I hear God speaking to me, and He told me to come over and ask you to pray for me." She told me that she was due to go into hospital in a matter of days for a serious operation, and the doctors were not too sure that it would be successful. The lady told me how nervous she had been feeling, how she had asked God to do something for her and then she had heard this voice telling her to ask me to pray. I suggested that we walked back to the police station, where we would be able to pray quietly in one of the interview rooms. I did not pray for very long, but asked God for His healing and His blessing on the lady, and then I had to get back on duty.

The lady came back about a week later. Her husband had taken her into hospital on his way to work the day before the operation as planned. He promised to come back and visit her that evening. So when he finished

49

work he bought some flowers for his wife, then hurried home to change before he went to the hospital. But when he got home he found his wife laying the table for their evening meal. "What on earth are you doing here?" he asked.

His wife explained that the doctor had examined her in the morning, then called over another doctor. "I began to think something must be very seriously wrong. Soon there was a group of doctors around my bed, including the surgeon and the consultant. Eventually they told me that they could not find anything wrong, so they sent me home."

I did not know what to think when I heard this story. Was God starting to use me in the healing ministry? "I do not know what is going on, Lord," I prayed, "But if you want to use me in this ministry, well you could not have chosen a bigger fool than me. I shall make all sorts of mistakes unless you help me all the time."

A few months later I found myself driving to Swindon to take a healing service. I had been to a service in Oxford the previous week, and at the end the preacher had come over to speak to the man I was talking to and, explaining that he had somehow managed to accept two different bookings for the same evening, he asked the other man if he would take one for him. The two men obviously knew each other well, but neither of them knew me at all, so I was staggered when the second man turned to me and said, "This is the man who should take the service for you." Hardly realising what I was doing I had agreed.

I spent most of my free time that week preparing my talk. It was a simple message, telling the good news of Jesus. I said to God, "If this service is the kind of ministry you want me to do, then I want at least ten people to become Christians and all those I pray for to be instantly healed on this visit to Swindon.'' I was putting out a fleece that night, just as Gideon put out his fleece in the Bible to check whether or not God really wanted to use him. I knew it was rather a cheek to talk to God like that, but I was asking for what for me was impossible, so that He could guide me clearly through what happened.

When I arrived at the school where the service was going to be held there were only 35 people in the room. It seemed very unlikely that more than 10 out of such a small number would become Christians. If there had been a hundred it might have seemed more likely. I gave my talk as planned, and at the end I asked people to come right out to the front to give their hearts to Jesus. Fourteen people came forward — God had met the first part of my 'fleece'. Then I invited those who were sick to come forward for prayer. There were 17, half the congregation.

I went along the line, praying for each one in turn. Immediately each one was miraculously healed. A deaf man could hear again, a blind lady could see. I came to a young girl, who told me she was an epileptic. ''When did you last have a fit?'' I asked. She looked a bit surprised. ''I don't think you understand how bad my problem is; I have an average of 10 fits each day.'' I had never prayed for something like this before, and I did not know how to pray, so I asked the Holy Spirit to guide my prayers. Then I laid hands on her and asked God to heal her completely, and to set her free from everything that bound her. I asked the Holy Spirit to guide me in my prayer, and I concluded with the words; ''Jesus breaks every fetter and sets you free tonight.'' I remember hearing a sound like a bunch of keys falling on the floor as I prayed, but it did not seem very

51

significant.

As I finished praying for the final person, the epileptic girl came up to me. She asked if I had heard something fall on the floor as I prayed. "This was what it was", she said, holding up a chain-link bracelet. On the plate of the bracelet was her name and address, and the words 'severe epileptic'. When I prayed for her one of the metal links holding the name plate in the chain had broken, as though it had been cut through quite cleanly, and the bracelet had fallen off her wrist. It seemed a sign that God had freed her from the epilepsy as well. When I saw the girl six months later she was able to confirm this; she had not suffered from a single fit since I prayed for her. God had indeed healed every one of the seventeen people at Swindon.

I retired from the police force aged 47 and started a job working for a security firm. This involved travelling long distances, as I was covering an area from Bristol to East Anglia. This could prove very useful, as sometimes I was invited to take healing services, and I could arrange my work schedule to put me in the right place at the right time. As I had to spend so much time in the car, I tried to pray as I drove, to make the most of the time. God quite often used my travelling to bring me into contact with people to whom he wanted me to minister, and who I would never have come across in my normal life.

One day I was driving home after a business meeting in High Wycombe. It was quite late in the afternoon, and I was keen to get home as soon as I could because I had to go out again to a prayer meeting near Oxford that evening. When I had been driving for about fifteen minutes I glanced down and noticed a pair of glasses on the passenger seat. They did not belong to me, and I suddenly realised what had happened. I had been about to leave the firm in High Wycombe, when one of the people I had been to see suddenly remembered something he wanted to say to me. He had stopped me in the car park, and stood talking to me through the window. I remembered him taking off his glasses, and fiddling with them as we talked. He must have dropped them on to the passenger seat without me noticing, and I had driven off with them. What a nuisance! I did not know whether to take them back to him, or whether to go on home. If I went back I would be late for the prayer meeting, but the man might desperately need his glasses. I thought I had better take them back, so turned the car round and headed back to High Wycombe. The man was very grateful, and I set off again on the road without losing too much time. When I reached the spot where I had originally noticed the glasses and turned the car around I saw a man smartly dressed in grey flannel trousers and a check jacket standing on the side of the road trying to hitch a lift.

I never normally stopped to pick up hitch-hikers, but I sensed that God wanted me to stop for this man. As I drew up beside him, and he climbed into the car I noticed that he was wearing a clerical collar. I had picked up a vicar! I told him it was rather unusual to find a vicar hitch-hiking, and asked if he was a local man, and where he wanted to go. I told him that I was on my way to Oxford for a prayer meeting, and could take him as far as that. The vicar told me that he was from Coventry but he was on his way to visit a young girl from his congregation who was in hospital in Birmingham with a tumour on the brain. She was going to have an operation the following day, and the doctors had told her parents that there was only one chance in ten that she would pull through. Her parents had asked the vicar to give their daughter Holy Communion the night before the operation, and he was on his way to the hospital now.

"If you are from Coventry, and this girl is in hospital in Birmingham, then what are you doing near High Wycombe?" I asked. The vicar explained that his wife was recuperating in Kent after a serious operation. "Yesterday she had a relapse, and they sent for me. I set off straight away, but when I got as far as Stratford-upon-Avon the exhaust fell off the car. I had to leave the car there and hitch a lift the rest of the way."

I asked if his wife was better. "Not really," he replied. "I did not want to leave her, but I had promised to visit this girl in Birmingham."

I told him that I was on my way to a prayer meeting. "We regularly pray for the sick and see God heal them, and if you would like we will pray for your wife and the sick girl tonight." When I asked him a few more questions he told me that he had only been waiting for a few seconds before I stopped to pick him up. If I had not gone back to High Wycombe with the pair of glasses I would not have met him. This seemed like one of God's coincidences to me. I dropped him at Oxford station, where he could catch a train direct to Birmingham. As he got out of the car we swopped our names and addresses, and I promised to pray for the two women at our prayer meeting.

About ten days later I received a letter from the vicar:

Dear Fred,

Thank you for praying for the girl in my church with the tumour on the brain. She did not have her operation after all. When they came to prepare her for the operation on the morning after I met you there was no sign of the tumour. I am writing to you from the office at church, and downstairs the children are having a party. I can hear the shrieks of joy as I write. At the moment the girl for whom you prayed is leading them in a game of 'Follow My Leader'!

P.S. Thank you too for praying for my wife. I heard today that she is making a miraculous recovery and will soon be back at home.

It was marvellous news. I only wondered what had happened to their car stuck in Stratford.

On another occasion I was on my way to London with four friends for a meeting one evening in the Spring of 1965 when one of the tyres burst. The car was nearly new — I had only done a few thousand miles in it, and the tyre should not have punctured like this; however we reached the meeting in time and parked the car near-by. When we came out afterwards it was nearly 11.30pm, and I was longing to get home. As we reached the car I saw to my horror and astonishment that there was another flat tyre. We had parked in Vauxhall Bridge Road, near Victoria Station, and there was no garage in sight. I would have to get one of the tyres repaired, as the spare tyre was already on the car. I did not know London very well, and I had no idea where the nearest garage was, nor whether it would be open at that time of night. Suprisingly for London there was no sign of a public phonebox, and there were very few cars around, so there was no one I could ask for help.

"Lord, I do not know what to do. Please help us" I prayed. Just at that moment the front door of one of the houses opposite opened, and a man came out carrying some empty milk bottles. I went over and explained my problem to him. It turned out that he was a chauffeur, and he very kindly asked me in and let me use his telephone. I rang the motoring organisation I belong to, but I had just missed the midnight deadline, and there was no reply. So the chauffeur produced a couple of telephone directories and we started ringing local garages until we found one willing to mend my tyre. I thanked the man for his kindness and set off with one of my friends, bowling the tyre down the roads for about half a mile until we got to the garage. By the time the tyre was repaired, and we were back at the car with the wheel changed it was after half-past one in the morning before we left London.

Next morning I came down to breakfast rather sleepily and picked up my glasses off the table to read the newspaper. My eyes tried to focus, but even in my sleepy state I knew these were not my glasses. "Stella, where did you find these glasses?" I called to my wife in the kitchen. "They were in your jacket pocket as usual." she replied. I reached over to my jacket lying over the back of a chair where I had hung it the night before, and put my hand into the pockets. Nothing in the first one but in the other, my glasses. Where had I got this other pair from?

I could remember using my glasses to look up the telephone numbers of garages the night before. The chauffeur helping me had also been wearing glasses, and I realised that I must have put my glasses back in-to my pocket, and then seeing a pair on the table I absent-mindedly picked his up as well. I did not know the man's name, or the number of his house, but I would obviously have to take the glasses back and try to find him. Luckily I did not have anything planned for that morning, so I drove straight back to London.

When I got to Vauxhall Bridge Road I parked the car about where I thought I had parked the night before. I looked across at the row of houses. There was nothing to make me recognise one from the others. I did not remember seeing a number, and it had been too dark even to distinguish the colour of the door. "Lord, I do not know what to do now. Please help me to find the right house" I prayed. The door to one of the houses opened, and the man I had met the night before came out. He looked up and down the street, then went back inside. What a clear answer!

I rang the doorbell, and stood waiting on the doorstep. He recognised me at once and said, "You have got my spectacles haven't you?" I gave them back to him, and apologised, explaining what must have happened. "I am sorry it has taken me so long to get back, but I had to come up from Oxford," I explained.

"Have you come all the way from Oxford to bring back my glasses? Come in and have a cup of coffee before you drive all the way back again." I went inside and he made some coffee and we started to talk. When he asked me what I had been doing in London the night before I started to talk about God. I asked the man whether he ever went to church? "Well, not for a long while now," he said.

Then the doorbell rang. "That will be my wife. Excuse me while I go and help her in." He disappeared for a few minutes and came back with a badly crippled woman on crutches. "Is this why you brought me back here, Lord?" I prayed silently. This looked like another of God's coincidences. We carried on chatting for a while, then I told them that I believed that God did not want anyone to be sick, and that Jesus had died to destroy sin and sickness. I asked if I could pray for the woman, and laid hands on her in the name of Jesus. She was completely healed from the pain and effects of disease, and they both gave their hearts to the Lord. When I met them again a couple of years later it was marvellous to see them fit and full of joy in the Lord.

God seems to go to a lot of trouble to reach people who need him. Sometimes it causes me quite a lot of inconvenience, like having to drive all the way back to London. But it was worth it to be involved in what God was doing.

Cutting through the village of Wheatley just outside of Oxford on my way between two business meetings I realised that I had left my briefcase behind. I am not usually a forgetful man, and today I had very little time to spare. I had just reached the crossroads in the centre of the village, so I turned round and headed up the hill out into the country again. When I was a little way up the hill I passed a gypsy slowly carrying a large petrol can up the the hill. As I drove past him I heard God tell me to stop and pick him up. "But Lord," I said, "I am late already, and it is against company policy to pick people up, and he looks so dirty!" I had a brand new company car, with smart red upholstery, and I was very proud of it. But I knew that it would be better to obey God, and not worry about the car seats. So I headed back into Wheatley, drove back to the crossroads to turn the car round again, and drew up by the gypsy. He was sitting on his petrol can, and looked up in surprise when I stopped the car.

"Would you like a lift?" I called out. "Yessir, thank you sir," and he scrambled into the car, petrol can and all, as though he was worried that I would drive off without him. He was breathing quite heavily, as though very out of breath from climbing the hill, and did not seem very fit. He was even dirtier than I had thought! "Have you run out of petrol?" I asked, for something to say. It turned out that he was out collecting scrap metal, and his lorry had run out of petrol just over the brow of the hill. As we came over the top I could see his wife and several children leaning against a lorry about half a mile further on. I slowed down and stopped. "I will take you on in a minute, but first I want to talk to you." I explained. I told him that I had driven passed him at first, and then come back to collect him. "I thought you did sir" he wheezed. I told him that I thought God had told me to stop for him. "Oh, I say my prayers regular like" he grinned. "God has used me to pray for people who are sick, and he heals them," I told him. "You seem to need some help — would you let me lay hands on you and pray for you now in the car?" He told me that he had severe heart trouble, and was very short of breath but that he believed that God could heal him. Then he whipped off his cap and I prayed for him. When I had finished his face was wreathed in smiles. "Thank'ee sir," he said. "I reckon I will be all right now."

I drove on towards his lorry, and pulled up about a hundred yards away. "You would never had been able to run that far, would you? Well you can get out now and run." He did. Not a stagger or pause, he ran straight and strong all the way back to his family. His wife shouted at him to stop being stupid, but he carried on. As I drove past I saw him reach them, not even out of breath. Yet again God had done something very remarkable for someone quite ordinary and in need. The whole meeting had taken less than ten minutes, but the gypsy's life would never be the same. I drove on, wondering what would happen on my next travelling encounter.

5

The Town Hall Meetings

"Fred, you are always going off to minister in different parts of the country. Why don't we hold some special services here in Oxford? Somewhere neutral so that people don't feel put off by a church building. Somewhere big so that we can get everyone in."

The idea came from one of our church members, but we were all excited about it. Although I have been invited to minister in churches all over the country I have always enjoyed opportunities to minister in my own home area. I am now the pastor of the New Testament Church, Oxford, and we meet regularly on Sunday evenings at St Matthew's Church in South Oxford. These services are always open to anyone who would like to come along, but we have also held healing services in Oxford over the last few years aimed specifically for outsiders.

The services would be just like many other services that I have ministered at over the past years. But on these occasions it was our fellowship organising the evening. When I am invited to speak at a meeting in a church or hall anywhere in the country I only have to get myself ready and turn up and minister as God leads me. But we had to organise everything for the Oxford services.

I spent some time praying about our intended outreach, asking God to guide me about all the details. As I prayed God spoke plainly, "Take the Town Hall for 3 consecutive nights." One way to test whether or not this was the Lord speaking would be to see if I would be able to make a booking. When I went along to the Town Hall I was told it was fully booked for the next six months. "Well, I was wanting to book it for three nights in October. Please will you just check to see if there are any free evenings?" The bookings clerk flicked through the pages, right to the end of the month. "There has been a cancellation, so the hall is free the 30th and 31st October, and these are the only two consecutive free in the whole month," she told me. Two nights would be better than nothing, but God had said three nights. "Please will you check again, and see whether the next evening is also free?" I asked. The clerk turned over the page. "It just happens that November 1st is also free — I did not think to turn over to November since you had specifically asked for October — so you can have the three consecutive evenings." We decided to go ahead.

First and foremost I see myself as an evangelist. I long to see people accept Jesus into their lives, to put right their relationship with him, and receive his forgiveness, and enter into a new life with his Holy Spirit. I believe that praying for the sick is important too, and it is exciting when God heals someone and this sign of His power brings that person and others to faith in God. This seems to be the way that Jesus ministered. We are told that he was 'full of compassion' for the sick, that he performed miracles and healings and then taught the people about God. In the Acts of the Apostles we see the disciples following this pattern. Healing was often a sign and demonstration of God's power, added to the disciples' preaching and many people became Christians as a result.

When I am ministering away from home I may pray for people and never see them again. Sometimes I will get letters from the person telling me of their healing, or hear from the local vicar about people joining his church having become Christians. But the services at Oxford Town Hall were opportunities for me to keep in contact with those we prayed for, and I have watched people receive healing, come to faith in God and have their lives dramatically changed.

Hilary Windows is one such person. Brought up in Oxford she lived abroad for some time and on her return home from Australia she met a friend who encouraged her to 'search for the truth'. I met her in October 1977, and later she told me her story.

"It all started from a book I was reading about the power of positive thinking. It was about how to make the best of my life, but it was all to do with me, my efforts and my thoughts and nothing about God. I started to turn my back on my Christian upbringing, and soon I was involved in the occult and esoteric experiences. Life was not fulfilling, which may be why I felt so attracted to the idea of reincarnation — if things in this life seemed hard maybe I would come back as a princess in the next life. For ten years I carried on my search for truth, but I could not find it. Instead I had a horrible out of body experience and I was tormented with thoughts about evil spirits so that I was always frightened at night. Regular visits to a spiritist medium only left me more frightened.

"Then in the summer of 1977 I started to feel intense pain in my shoulders and elbows. My hands started to swell and I started to feel as though I had raging toothache in my shoulders, elbows, hips, hands and gradually all over my body. The doctor diagnosed rheumatoid arthritis, and prescribed all kinds of drugs to deal with the swelling and the pain. Nothing seemed to deal with it. My hands and wrists were soon so swollen that I could not wear any jewellery or even a watch. By October I could not even hold a pen in my hand to write. My parents had to cut up my food, and help feed me; I could not hold a full cup of tea, or answer the telephone because the receiver was too heavy. Not only was it terribly painful to bend my joints, but I also felt as though I had no power in my hands. I was quite severly limited in what I could do, the disability was getting worse, and despite the drugs I was in pain 24 hours a day. I used to see the doctor about twice a week and he suggested manipulation and traction as well as more drugs.

"The pain never left, but it was brought to a manageable level by the drugs plus a pain killer every two and a half hours throughout the day. But as with so many drugs there were side effects, sometimes quite violent shaking, and then feeling sick and faint. It seemed crazy; I took the drugs to deal with the pain, but the sickness was almost worse than the pain. I took to sitting in the garden even in the autumn winds just for relief and the refreshment of the cold air. The nights were the worst times of all; when my family were all asleep I would be lying awake, my whole body wracked in pain. I was so tired that I longed to lie down and sleep, but when I lay on my bed it felt as though there were red hot knives searing through almost every joint in my body. I took to walking around the kitchen at dead of night, hoping that the sound of my sobbing would not wake the family. I had tried everything and nothing seemed to bring lasting relief.

"I felt so enclosed in the pain and disability that I wanted to die, but I was afraid of death. In my desperation I went with my mother to the local health food shop, not really knowing what I would find there, but hoping that some 'alternative medicine' would do something for me. Outside the shop I met a girl with whom I had worked ten years before. We had both been medical secretaries at the local hospital, but had lost touch when I left and went abroad. "Where are you working now?" asked Jeannie.

"That question opened the flood gates to all my anger and self pity. "Jeannie, I am in so much pain from arthritis that I keep my hands in my pocket to support my arms and take the pressure off my shoulders. I cannot move my hands more than a few inches, certainly not even up to my face. I cannot work — I could not do anything!" I retorted.

"Jeannie reacted very gently and calmly. She told me how she had recently been healed, and that she believed God could heal me too. 'You must come to hear Fred Smith at the Town Hall' she said.

"I was prepared to try anything once. I think that I would have stood on my head if it would have made any difference. So I said I would be interested in going with her. But I did not really expect to see her again. So many people had said, 'you must come to this, or hear this person or try this cure' but it had all been words and I had not heard from them again. I had become very cynical about broken promises. When Jeannie arrived to collect me on the first evening of the Town Hall meetings I suddenly did not want to go with her.

"She came back again the next night, and then I was

feeling terrible. I had tried a special 'stretching' technique called traction during the day, when I had been tilted right up and my head was held firmly so that my body weight pulled downwards, so stretching me. It eased the pain for a few hours but my head was swimming, and added to that I had taken an excessive dose of drugs to ease the discomfort, which left me feeling as if I was floating. I heard my father explaining to Jeannie that I was not feeling up to going out. "We could take her on a stretcher." Jeannie offered. I could hardly believe my ears. What a mad idea! "Get that fanatical woman out of here," I told my father. "I do not want to go. Doesn't she realise that I am sick?"

"I suppose it was because I was sick that Jeannie kept trying. I realise now that it was God's love and compassion in Jeannie that made her persevere. When she arrived on the third evening she was very forthright. "Are you going to come tonight? This is your last chance!" I thought I had better take it, so my mother and Jeannie helped me into the car. When we got to the Town Hall my heart sank. All those stairs up to the hall. It was far worse than an ordinary flight of stairs, probably twice as far. I would never manage them on my own. Jeannie and Mother gently encouraged me, and eased me up, step by step. My body jarred with each movement.

"When the meeting started things went from bad to worse as far as I was concerned. There was an organ near where we were sitting, and someone came over and started playing. I could see these stickers on his belongings, 'Smile, Jesus loves you!' What kind of loopy Christian fringe was this? The hymns and songs we were singing were so soppy. I would not sing — that was my protest — and if it had not been for the thought of all those stairs I might have left there and then. I could not even get out past Jeannie who had carefully sat at the end of the row. I felt trapped. To make matters worse Jeannie leant across and said to me, "By the way, we are Pentecostals!" That was like a dirty word to me. It must mean the service would be wild and quite over the top. What had I come to?

"Then Fred Smith stood up and started to speak. I was very angry, because almost at once he started to warn people against the dangers of spiritism, saying that the occult controlled peoples' lives in order to destroy them, and that it was evil and wrong. I was furious. He was talking about my friends! I mean, who does this man think he is? I was so busy being angry that I did not listen to the rest of the sermon. Then I heard Fred say, "....give your hearts to Jesus." Suddenly my anger evaporated and all I knew was that I had to get up to the front and respond. I did not know why, but I did know that I wanted to give my heart to the Lord.

"To my embarrassment, when I got up to the front I saw someone I recognised. Now all Oxford will know about this! I do not know how I managed to stand there. But now I am so glad that I did stay. First Fred prayed a prayer for us to echo, giving our lives to God. Then after he had dealt with everyone wanting to become a Christian he invited people to go forward for prayer for healing. I joined the queue at once; by now I had nothing to lose.

"I watched as Fred prayed for a Spanish woman in front of me. To my surprise she slumped to the ground, as if she had fainted. I wondered what kind of impact this man had on people. I saw someone catch her as she fell, and lay her gently on the floor. But it was the expression on her face that most intrigued me. Before she reached Fred she had looked drawn and anxious, but when he laid hands on her and she went down her whole expression changed; her cheeks were rosy, she looked as peaceful as though she was in heaven. Even so I was determined this was not going to happen to me. I was wearing my best skirt and I did not want to end up on the dirty floor. I might be sick but I was not stupid.

"When Fred came over to me, he looked at me and simply said "God has saved your soul; now he is going to heal your body." That was the first positive thing anyone had said in the three months since the arthritis started: when I spoke to the doctor he would not look me in the eye, and could give me no hope. In contrast Fred simply placed his hands on my head and spoke to a spirit of arthritis, commanding it to leave me. I did not understand what that meant, but I did know that at that moment the pain became a hundred times worse. I wanted to scream with pain. Then suddenly there was the most amazing power coming through the top of my head. It is almost impossible to describe, but as this 'power' hit my body the pain left, and I felt warmth and a sense of well-being flood through my whole body. I can only explain it as a tangible feeling of the power of God actually touching my body. I believed that it was God because Fred had asked God to heal me. I found I did not want to stand any longer, and best skirt or no best skirt I flopped back. I felt someone catch me and lay me on the floor. I was not unconscious, I could hear people talking around me, but the sensation of warmth and wellbeing was so pleasant that I was quite happy staying where I was.

"After a few minutes Fred came over and helped me to my feet. "In the name of Jesus, raise your arms!" he said. I knew I could not do anything of the sort. For nearly four months I had only been able to raise my hands a few inches. But as I started to raise my arms, in some way believing that God had indeed touched my body, I found that I could raise my arms above my head without pain. All the heaviness had gone, and all the mobility was back in my joints, and I could move my arms round and round. I felt the most incredible joy. Becoming a Christian and being touched by God in this way was the most exciting experience of my life.''

Hilary was only one of many people we saw healed on that night, but that was not the end of her story. Although Hilary never lost her mobility she did begin to experience some pain again, and her first thought was that God had not worked after all, just as every other attempt to cure her had failed. But her friend Jeannie was still praying for her, and throughout the next few days God would prompt Jeannie to phone Hilary and pray with her over the phone whenever the pain came back. It was a remarkable situation. Jeannie seemed to know whenever Hilary was in pain, and when she phoned up and they prayed the pain left her again.

After another appointment at the doctor Hilary was told that there was nothing much wrong with her, just some residual weakness in the shoulders. As she came out of the hospital Hilary turned to her parents, and said ''It was not God healing me after all, just some kind of electric shock.'' From that moment the pain started to come back, and her condition deteriorated until she was back where she had started. Somehow, by denying her healing, it was as though, in the spiritual realm, she was allowing the sickness back. Jeannie tried to explain it to her, and Hilary came back to God, and back to the church, where people prayed for her week after week. Her progress was slow but definite, and after nearly a year she was completely fit again. Now, nearly nine years later Hilary's whole life has been transformed. She describes it as going from an empty life without meaning to an exciting life with the Lord, knowing His power in her life. In the church we see her used again and again, coming alongside those who are in trouble, praying for the sick and seeing them healed, showing God's love to those in need, praying with them, and supporting them, just as Jeannie supported her.

Hilary's story illustrates the different ways that God will heal. Sometimes it is instantaneous, and people receive healing once and for all. Other times we will pray again and again, and see a very little progress each time. There is nothing wrong with praying for someone more than once. When Jesus healed the blind man *(Mark 8, 24)* he laid his hands on the man, and at first he could see 'men, but they look like trees walking', so Jesus laid his hands on him a second time and the man's sight was fully restored. That story always encourages me to keep on praying if we do not see an immediate answer to prayer. I do not understand why it is like this, but perhaps sometimes there are things we need to sort out with God before we can receive healing. But one thing I have learnt is that God deals with us as the different individuals we are, with our different problems and needs, even if the outward physical signs of illness are similar.

In Hilary's case when she gave her life to Jesus and I prayed the first time she received complete healing. Later she seemed to lose that healing, and when we prayed for her regularly over the next year there were times when she repented of her occult involvement, and cutting her free from these influences we saw the healing process increase. But not all cases of arthritis are the same as Hilary's, nor do we always pray in the same way.

Another lady came to the Town Hall for prayer for

70

bad arthritis, and from the outside it seemed a similar situation. Another woman crippled by a painful disease, believing that God could heal her, and wanting prayer. But when she came up to me and I started to ask her one or two questions I began to realise that this was very different. It was as though the Holy Spirit spoke to me and told me that the woman's arthritis was connected to some unforgiveness in her life. I believe that in every situation there is a root cause of sickness — either spiritual, emotional or physical, and for there to be healing we have to deal with the root cause. So instead of praying for her I talked to her further.

"Is there someone that you have said you will never forgive?" I tried to ask the question gently, but from the look on her face it was obvious at once that this was right. "It's my husband" she whispered. I looked at the man with her; had I just caused an embarrassing situation, and possibly caused trouble in the marriage? The lady must have understood my expression. "Not this husband, my first husband!" she explained. Twenty years ago her first husband had left her, and subsequently emigrated to Canada, and she had been so hurt by the break up of their marriage that she had never forgiven him.

"Look, my dear," I said. "I hope you will forgive me for speaking quite plainly to you, but it seems to me that God told me about your unforgiveness because it is in some way connected to your arthritis. We could pray for you now and ask God to heal you and maybe He would, but we would not have dealt with the root cause, and probably within a month you would be back in the same situation. In all these years your ex-husband has probably hardly even thought about you, and your unforgiveness may not have affected him at all, but it is destroying you. It is so important to be able to forgive

71

people who have hurt us, however badly we have been treated. Think about what you say in the Lord's Prayer; "Forgive us our sins as we forgive those who sin against us …." Forgive us as we forgive — that's like making an agreement with God. Please forgive me the same way and to the extent that I forgive others. So if you do not forgive your husband it is as though you are asking God not to forgive you. If we refuse to forgive we are not able to accept God's forgiveness ourselves. I believe that we then open ourselves to the influence of unforgiving spirits which are able to attack our body through the arthritis. Don't you think it is time you dealt with this?"

I sent the couple away, suggesting that the lady asked God to help her forgive her first husband, and then come back for prayer the next evening. I had tried to speak kindly and gently, but it was a sensitive matter and I knew that only God could help this woman to forgive her husband. I believed that God indeed wanted to help and heal this woman. When through His Holy Spirit He gives us knowledge that we could not possibly have — the Bible calls this a Word of Knowledge — it is often a sign that he wants to do something special for someone.

The next evening the couple were back. She was still badly crippled, and had to hold onto her husband as they came up to me. But this time her face was different. She no longer looked bowed down with her troubles, she was at peace with herself. "It took most of the night," she told me. "But in the end, with God's help, I was able to forgive and to receive God's forgiveness for myself. Now I want you to pray for my physical healing." As I asked God to touch this lady and heal her, I realised just what a loving, powerful God we serve. He cared enough for that one woman, out of the many people in the Town Hall to help her to forgive, and then to heal her body as well as her heart.

6

Dinah Hills

In the book of Acts we have the story of Dorcas (the Greek name for Tabitha; both names are used in the Bible), who fell ill and died. After her death, the Christians in Joppa sent for Peter to come from the nearby town.

"When he arrived, he was taken to the room upstairs, where all the widows crowded round him, crying and showing him all the shirts and coats that Dorcas had made while she was alive. Peter put them all out of the room, and knelt down and prayed; then he turned to the body and said, "Tabitha, get up!" She opened her eyes, and when she saw Peter she sat up .... The news about this spread all over Joppa and many people believed in the Lord."

This very dramatic healing had a dramatic effect on the local community. A few years ago I met someone whose story seems to have had a similar effect. Her name was not Dorcas, but Dinah.

Dinah Hills was a professional dressmaker. One day in 1972 when she was visiting a client she slipped and fell on a highly polished parquet wood floor. The pain in her left arm was excruciating. A trip to the local hospital for X-rays confirmed that she had broken her left wrist. But even after several days in plaster Dinah was still in great pain. "Surely a broken wrist should not hurt so much once it is in plaster." she said to her husband, Roy. The pain became unbearable, so Roy took her back to the hospital, and the doctor extended the plaster up to her elbow to give extra support. Six weeks later the X-rays showed that the broken wrist bones had mended, and the plaster came off. But Dinah was still suffering great pain from an injury that was meant to be better.

Over the next few months Dinah's doctor tried to find out what was wrong. He gave her pain killers which did something for the pain, but he could not treat her for a broken bone when the bone was healed, and nothing else showed up on the X-rays. But it was clear that something was still wrong. Not only was the pain excruciating, but Dinah's arm started to turn black, as though it was very badly bruised, but the bruises did not fade, and her fingers started to curl inwards as the muscles wasted away. The slightest touch on her arm caused Dinah great pain. She cut the sleeves out of her dresses, and sat in a chair at night because she could not even bear the feel of any material against her arm.

Dinah was sent to one specialist after another. Eventually one suggested an operation. "Your ulnar nerve is trapped. We should be able to put it right with a simple operation, and you will just have a small scar." But when he came round to see Dinah after the operation with his registrar the surgeon admitted that it had been much more complicated than he had expected. Two of the main nerves in the arm, the ulnar nerve and the median nerve were both trapped. These two nerves control all the fingers of the hand, which was why

Dinah's fingers were curling up. Her arm was turning black because the blood supply was not getting through properly. The two trapped nerves had the effect of an exposed nerve in a tooth, so it was no wonder Dinah was in constant pain. "How did you put up with the pain?" asked the registrar after the operation. "I had to," was the only reply.

The operation was a partial success, but Dinah was still living with pain. Next she tried acupuncture, and this treatment deadened the pain, but the acupuncturist told her that he could not cure the cause of the pain. Eventually a nursing friend told Dinah of an Australian surgeon who was in England for a few weeks. He agreed to operate, and created a new tracking for the nerve which seemed to solve the problem. A few months later it felt as though the new tracking was giving way and the pain was back, as bad as ever. When she visited another specialist, to see if he could repair the nerve tracking he told her that there was nothing he could do and that these operations had only one chance in a hundred of success.

The next treatment was an attempt to block the nerves. "It was like holding sparklers in each hand, while an electric current passed between them. I felt like a child at play, watched by two specialists. But it did nothing for me." The doctors tried again to control her pain. She was sent to the cancer clinic in Abingdon for pain killing injections. Sometimes she felt so odd and 'woozy' after taking painkillers that she could hardly walk across the room, but even these did not stop the pain. In the end one London specialist promised that if all else failed he would cut the nerve; this would reduce the pain, but also impair sensation. As far as Dinah was concerned it would be worth anything if only she could be out of pain.

Dinah saw yet another specialist who told her that if the man in London could not do anything then there was nothing anyone could do. "He is the leading man on arms. If you had broken every bone in your body we could have done more for you, but with nerves we are just scratching the surface." It was now several years after Dinah's accident, and she had seen ten specialists, had two operations, endless treatment from physiotherapists and acupuncturists, and the 'sparkler' blocking treatment. Eventually Dinah was sent for a new set of tests.

"The blood supply in your arm is restricted at your wrist, your elbow and at the top of the arm." The results showed that there was nothing more they could do; they could not cut the nerve to end the pain for fear of gangrene. Dinah would be in this pain for the rest of her life. "When I heard this I wanted to jump out of the hospital window."

It was not just the pain, but the disability which was so terrible; her arm and hand were in effect useless. Roy arranged to take early retirement to be at home to help Dinah. He had to help dress her, and do most of the practical chores, because Dinah really only had the use of one hand. "You would be surprised how many people touch you on the arm when they greet you" Dinah explained. The pain would make her want to scream. Going out, even for a meal, was a major problem. If Dinah went to the ladies' cloakroom she would warn Roy to send someone to find her if she was away for long. The heavy springs on the doors, which acted as a fire precaution were far too heavy for her to hold, and if she did not manage to keep it open with her foot Dinah could find herself stuck.

Seven years and one month after her accident Dinah was looking through the local paper when she saw an advertisement for one of the healing services at Oxford Town Hall. "Jesus Heals Today!" the caption read. Even the smallest possibility of healing was worth trying for Dinah. After ten specialists she was ready to try God. She decided to go along, and Roy came too.

I sometimes feel that I have an impossible task at a healing service. In the course of one talk I need to tell people about God, about Jesus' death on the Cross for their sins, the importance of putting things right with God — repenting of our sins — and tell them stories of how God has healed today to encourage their faith. I do not remember exactly what I said on that particular evening, but both Roy and Dinah decided to commit their lives to God. When it came to praying for the sick I had to go out of the hall to pray for Dinah. She had trouble breathing and had left the hall, but asked if I would come out to pray for her. I remember seeing her sitting waiting for me, with a jacket flung over her shoulders for warmth, because she could not bear putting her arm into the sleeve. Her arm was so shrunken and small it looked like a child's arm. I knew there was a queue of people waiting for me inside the hall, so I did not have time to ask many questions. I laid my hands on her head, and prayed for God to heal her arm and take away the pain. As with so many others, Dinah was overwhelmed with the power of the Holy Spirit and lay on the ground looking so peaceful she was almost glowing.

The next Sunday Dinah and Roy came to our church service. Dinah told me that the pain had gone as soon as I prayed for her, and for the next three days she had sat waiting for it to come back. After more than seven years it was hard to believe the pain had finally gone (her breathing problem was also healed). They were both so excited, and so grateful for what God had done.

Dinah's arm still looked wasted and child-like, so after the service that Sunday evening I prayed for her again. This time I commanded the muscles to fill out, and repair what was damaged. There were no signs that evening that anything was happening, but we believed that God would complete the healing He had begun.

Within two weeks Dinah's arm was fully restored. It was the same size and shape as the other, with only a six-inch scar from one of the operations to remind her of what had been. She went back to her own doctor and showed it to him. "Well, whatever happened is a miracle, and if it is good enough for you it is good enough for me!" he exclaimed. Some time later I met one of Dinah's specialists at dinner at her home. He too had no explanation, and agreed that it could only be a miracle.

Dinah and Roy lived in a small village not far from Oxford, and they were well known in the area. They wanted to tell everyone about what had happened to them, and they asked me if I would take a service in the local village hall. They put leaflets about the service through every door, and told everyone they could. When I arrived at the hall there was nowhere to park my car. There were three hundred people there that evening, and over eighty of them accepted Christ as their Saviour. I was invited to return the following week, and another sixty-eight people became Christians on that occasion.

On one of these evenings a young Australian girl in a wheel-chair came up to the front of the hall. She told me that her spine had been crushed in a serious car accident, and she had been told that she would never be able to walk again. "Do you believe that you can be healed?" I asked her. It was hard for her, having been told that there was no hope, she now could hardly bear to hope in case she was disappointed. She nodded her agreement. I put my hands on the top of her spine and started to pray. I asked God to remake her spine, to repair the damage that had been done in the accident, and to restore all her mobility. I believe that God made each one of us, so he can remake what has been destroyed. I prayed over each part of her spine, moving my hands slowly down her back. I had not even reached the bottom of her spine when the girl suddenly leapt up out of her wheel-chair and started walking away. "Come back!" I called. She was beaming all over her face. "When were you last able to walk like this?" I asked. "Not since before my accident", she replied, and turned to walk off with her husband, leaving the empty wheel-chair behind. I had never seen anyone so nonchalant about their healing. The couple were so excited that they walked out of the hall without a backward glance. There was no sign of any gratitude to God, and I wonder whether she fully understood what God, out of his great love and mercy for her had done for her. Whatever her reaction, we were excited.

The news of Dinah's healing had spread through the area. The two evening meetings in their village hall reminded me of what happened in Dorcas' village in the Bible. "The news spread all over Joppa, and many people believed in the Lord." *(Acts 9:42)*. We had seen that come true for ourselves. We cannot argue when a withered arm has been healed. We cannot say that we have imagined it, or that it was getting better anyway. After two operations and endless treatment, ten specialists had not been able to do anything for Dinah. But when God touched her she was healed completely, and back at her dressmaking for the first time in seven years. A month after she was healed she made a beautiful and intricate wedding dress for a friend. Her

80

healing was indeed complete, and her livelihood restored.

I think that sometimes we imagine that becoming a Christian and receiving healing is the end of the story. But for Roy and Dinah it was only the beginning. They became fully involved in our church fellowship, and soon Roy became one of a small group of people who would join me in praying for the sick. He was the first person to pray for a lady who came forward for prayer at another Town Hall meeting five years ago.

Sheila Hughes had suffered from a slipped disc for over sixteen years. Her lower lumbar disc was worn out and kept moving about so much that it had worn to a fragment. A possible operation to fuse the spine would have left Sheila's back rigid, and when she was warned that it was likely that after a year the vertebra higher up in the spine would cause trouble she decided against having an operation.

Sheila and her husband Peter kept a pub in Oxford, and Sheila used to help out as much as she could. She did all the book work and the accounts, and every few weeks she would try serving customers. She would always pick the straight-sided glasses, because they were the lightest, but by the time she had filled three with beer she was in so much pain that she would have to go home and lie flat on the floor. She could not sit or stand for long, and spent much of her life lying on the living-room carpet.

Sheila had tried all sorts of treatment, and was an early guinea-pig for treatment at a new orthapaedic hospital. The last year before she came to the Town Hall was the best year, with acupuncture every five days giving her some relief. "My ambition was to last the extra two days to make it a week between treatments," she said. Although things had been a little better for the last year Sheila was getting desperate. She was taking very strong pain-killers; the next thing would be morphine. How long would this period of relative ease last? Sheila was getting older, and she was very worried about how badly her condition might deteriorate in old age.

"I was talking to the girls who helped in the pub, and I mentioned that I had seen a notice advertising a service of healing at the Town Hall. They encouraged me to go along, although none of them wanted to come with me." The girls' response encouraged Sheila to risk going — after all, what could she loose? Peter agreed to take her to the Town Hall, although he was very surprised. "You are going to a meeting? But you never go anywhere!" he said.

The Town Hall was very full that evening and Sheila sat near the back. She admitted afterwards that she did not understand much of what was said, and she was one of the last to come forward for prayer. "I sat on my chair as though I was stuck to it by treacle, scared to go forward in case I was recognised by anyone. Then I made up my mind; the slipped disc had been taken sixteen years out of my life, and tonight there was a chance it could get better.

"About eighty people came forward that night, and Fred prayed a communal prayer for God's power to each person. Then he said, 'Those of you who have been healed can go back to your seats now', and about forty people left. I was still standing there in terrible pain, not really knowing what was going on. All I knew was that I was still in pain, so somewhat in a daze I stayed where I was."

There were several of us praying for the sick that night, and it was Roy, Dinah's husband who went up to Sheila and prayed for her. "He put his hands on my head, and started to pray for my hip. I was frantic; I wanted to tell him it was my spine, not my hips, but I did not think I ought to interrupt. I went to sit down, feeling unusually emotional. I was so used to keeping my emotions in check because I did not want my children to see me crying, but now I felt terribly weepy. As I was sitting at the front I felt this sharp pain in my lumbar region. A friend who was at the service came over and asked me how I was feeling. 'Dreadful!' I replied. It was definitely worse than before prayer. My friend insisted that I should go forward for more prayer; ''Something is happening to you,'' she said.

"This time another member of the church prayed for me, and I was able to touch my toes. I went home feeling very uncertain about what had happened, and expecting to be unable to sleep because I had stretched some muscles when I bent to touch my toes. Instead I slept peacefully right through the night. I was used to waking up with severe cramps in my left leg, which sometimes confined me to bed for a couple of hours. The morning after the Town Hall meeting I woke with cramps in the other leg, and as I started to rub my calf I called out involuntarily for help, 'Jesus!' ''

Sheila was soon free from all pain, and able to move easily and freely. One of the girls from the pub was sick that day, and Sheila went down to the pub to help out. It was a very busy day, but she felt perfectly fit, and was able to cope. That evening she took a ride in her daughter's low-slung sports car — she had never been able to bend herself enough to sit inside it before her healing. For the next ten days Sheila did everything she had ever wanted to do, and even started to re-decorate the living room. Her husband Peter, worried that she was overdoing things was very cross with her. "Even if I do go wrong, at least I will have done all the things I have been longing to do for years,'' Sheila replied.

Two hours later the pain was back. I suppose her case was rather like Hilary Windows; she had in some way denied her healing, opening herself up to a renewed attack. The following morning she rang the friends she had seen at the Town Hall, and told them what had happened. ''You must come back to church tomorrow night and have someone pray for you again.'' Sheila's initial reaction was very negative. ''This God thing does not seem to have worked for me!'' Over the course of the day she started thinking further. Perhaps there was something in Christianity — after all, she had been free from pain for ten days. She decided to come to church on the Sunday to ask for more prayer.

''This time Fred prayed for me; 'Forgive this foolish daughter.' I asked why I was foolish, and he replied, ''You only need faith the size of a mustard seed...'' After he prayed I was again free from pain, and I went home begining to believe that God had indeed healed me. Next morning I woke again in agony. I spent most of the morning lying flat on the carpet, resisting Satan's attack, as I had been taught at church the previous evening. Peter could not understand what was happening to me; one day I was well, then I was sick again. 'I have been healed, and I will soon be free from pain,' I told him.''

By midday Sheila was free from pain, and she has not had any more trouble in the five years since her healing. She cancelled her next acupuncture appointment, and has never been back. Soon she was back working full time at the pub, and she told all her friends about her healing. Whenever I dropped in to see Sheila and Peter at the pub it would thrill me to find a little group of people waiting for me to pray with them. When

Jesus was alive on earth he was accused of mixing with publicans; Sheila is a modern day pub-keeper who goes round telling her customers all about what Jesus has done for her.

7

The Healing Ministry

I am often asked why some people are healed and others are not. Of course this is the unanswerable question and, as many others have said, if I knew the answer to that question I would be God. I may pray for fifty people on any one evening, and only hear from a small number that they have been healed. Many others may also have been healed, and I do not know of it, but undoubtedly some are not healed. Sometimes I hear people say that divine healing is an emotional con-trick, or that healing does not really happen, or that someone claims to be healed and after a few days they are just as sick as they were before prayer. I accept that sometimes people do claim or pretend healing that has not actually happened.

I always try to establish exactly what people can and cannot do before I pray for healing, in order to know whether, for example, raising an arm, or walking, or being able to see clearly through an eye shows that they have indeed been healed. If someone cannot see before we pray for them, and afterwards they can see to distinguish people, or count how many fingers I am holding up or whatever, then I assume that they have been healed. I do not believe that we should claim healing unless some measure of healing has occured, but whenever there is healing I believe that God is glorified.

The story of Blind Bartimaeus in Mark's Gospel, chapter 10 seems to illustrate a peculiar truth about God's healing work. Bartimaeus is sitting by the side of the road when Jesus comes to Jericho, and he starts to shout out, "Jesus! Son of David! Take pity on me!" *(verse 47ff)*. When Jesus calls him over he asks Bartimaeus what seems to be an unnecessary question: "What do you want me to do for you?" What would a blind man want? "Teacher," Bartimaeus answers, "I want to see again". The obvious answer to an un-obvious question. Then Jesus heals him. What was the point of asking the question? Why did Jesus not just lay hands on him and heal him immediately?

I believe that this story illustrates how important it is that we should really want what God has for us, His healing and His blessing. That also means wanting to put behind us the things in our lives that are wrong, and getting rid of the things in our lives which are not pleasing to God. The lady I met at the Town Hall needed to forgive her ex-husband before she could receive healing, and to ask God to forgive her for her lack of forgiveness (Chapter 5). She wanted to be healed, and she wanted to put things right, and God healed her. I have heard of people who have asked for prayer for healing (from me and other people), who seem to have been healed, then a few days or weeks later they are as bad as ever. Does this mean they were not healed? Was it all an emotional or psychological trick? I do not think so.

I attempt to explain these cases in two possible ways

(there may of course be other explanations as well). Sometimes the person wants to be healed from the sickness, but does not want to sort out his or her life. After they have been healed they want to continue to lead their lives just as they please. Perhaps they go back to some habitual sin — sexual sin, occult practices, cruelty, cheating or whatever — and they turn their back on God and His laws. I believe that all sickness comes ultimately from Satan, and Christians are protected from Satan's power because of the way that Jesus defeated Satan's greatest weapon — death — through his resurrection. But when we turn our backs on God, and choose to live and lives our own way we are stepping outside God's protection. Perhaps it is not surprising in these situations if sometimes sickness returns.

Sometimes I think people do not really want to be healed. This may seem a harsh and rather sweeping statement, and I do not mean to imply by it that if someone is not healed it is because they do not really want it. But sometimes there can be a real cost in healing. Someone who has been ill for years, with a loving caring family, may be afraid of what it would be like to have to look for a job again, or take on responsibility for their own lives. There may even be a financial and material cost, with lost social security allowances. But sometimes when God heals someone, the social services do not know how to react to the changed situation.

On a visit to Norfolk I met a man who had been severly injured in an accident. Because of his disability he received certain mobility allowances from the social services, including an invalid person's car. I prayed for him at a meeting and he was miraculously healed, to his and our great excitement. Shortly after this he took his invalid car back to the people at the social services who had allocated it to him. "I think you had better have this car back," he said. "I am not disabled any longer — I have been completely healed — so I suppose I am not entitled to a car any more." The man at the social services did not know what to do. His regulation about who qualified for benefits and cars did not make any provisions for cases when people were healed. "I think you had better keep the car anyway," he said.

I firmly believe that there can be no permenant victory in the lives of Christians until they have the clearest possible understanding of the extent to which Satan was stripped of all his power on the Cross. As children of God we have that victory over all satanic invasion of our lives — and that includes our health.

The creation story in the Bible tells us that God took Adam and Eve, and put them in charge of the Garden of Eden. *(Genesis 1:28)* "God blessed them and said multiply, and rule over every living thing." God made man ruler over the whole world. But by Genesis chapter 3 Satan tempts Eve to eat the forbidden fruit, and both she and her husband eat some of the fruit — having chosen to follow Satan rather than God they put themselves under his control as his followers. So mankind came under the domination of Satan, and with him came sickness, sin, disease and even death.

The good news is that Jesus has defeated Satan through his death on the cross. "Through death he might destroy him who has the power of death, that is, the devil, and deliver all those who through fear of death were subject to lifelong bondage" *(Hebrews 2: 12ff)*. The work of Calvary has potentially put the devil out of action. But he can still harm us because we have not fully understood the implications of Jesus' death on the cross. Satan has been stripped of all his power over

89

God's children, so any hold he has is as a ursurper. The devil has no right to any place in any Christian's life, and it is our position to challenge him. We need to proclaim the devil's defeat loud and clear.

I believe that all sickness comes from Satan, be it a headache, depression, cancer, multiple sclerosis, alcoholism or whatever. In Luke chapter 13 we read the story of the woman who comes to Jesus for healing. For eighteen years she has been bent over and "could not fully straighten herself"; it sounds rather like curveture of the spine. When Jesus prayed for her the woman was immediately healed in the middle of the synagogue. The officials were angry that this had happened on the Sabbath day. Jesus said, "Ought not this woman, a daughter of Abraham as she is, whom Satan has bound these 18 long years, have been released from this bond on the Sabbath day?" Bondage to sickness comes from Satan. When Peter preaches about Jesus' ministry on earth he says, "he was healing all who were oppressed by the devil" *(Acts 10:38)*. You only heal someone who is sick — Jesus healed all those on whom Satan put sickness.

I was visiting a church in Kettering not long ago, and they brought a woman in a wheel-chair to me for prayer. She told me that she had multiple sclerosis, and she had been in a wheel-chair for 18 years. She had no movement whatsoever. "You do remind me of the woman in the Bible" I told her. "She was in church, and you are in church; Jesus said Satan had bound her for 18 long years, you have been bound for 18 years; Jesus was there to touch her and heal her, and Jesus is here tonight to touch you and heal you. Can you believe that?" I laid my hands on her head, and I prayed, "In the name of Jesus of Nazareth I command this sickness to leave you, and in the name of Jesus Christ, rise up and walk!'' She got straight out of her wheelchair and could walk.

Then a lady who had been totally blind for seven years was brought to me. She could not even distinguish light and dark, but she believed that God was going to restore her sight. I laid my hands over her eyes and prayed for full healing, asking that she might have 20-20 vision. As I took my hands away I asked ''What colour is my hair?'' She said ''White!'' Then the whole congregation laughed as she took my face in her hands and said ''Oh, you are lovely!'' ''My dear, anything would look lovely if you have been blind for seven years,'' I replied.

The next person who came up was a woman cancer patient, in a chair bed. Her husband came with her, and he was crying as he told me that his wife was only expected to live for a few more days or weeks. I prayed for her and rebuked the spirit of cancer, stripping it of all its authority over her body by the power in Jesus' name and commanded it to go. Then I asked God to make good all the parts of her body affected by the cancer. She gave me a warm smile and her husband wheeled her away. She looked just the same as before I had prayed. But at the end of the service a man came rushing up to me and flung his arms round me; ''Thank you for praying for my wife,'' he said, ''She has been healed.'' ''Which was your wife?'' I asked. ''She was the lady in the chair bed who had cancer,'' he replied. ''I am afraid she did not look up to much when she left me.'' ''Well, look at her now, over there in the church porch''. He pointed at a woman standing talking to a group of people. It was a dramatic change in a short space of time. I wanted to get through the crowds to talk to her, to verify what had happened, but by the time I pushed my way through to the porch there was no trace of this woman.

I had been invited to stay the night at the rectory and when we got back we had a cup of tea and sat chatting for a while about the service. "It was exciting when that lady was healed of cancer," the rector's wife said. I told her how disappointed I was to have missed her after the service. "I saw her talking to someone in the porch, but by the time I got over there they had disappeared." "I was talking to her in the porch," replied the rector's wife, "then we went outside. We were running and walking round and round the churchyard, and she seemed completely well."

On a recent visit to Chichester I met a lady who had been confined to a wheelchair for twelve years with severe rheumatoid arthritis. She had a plastic support under her chin, and what looked like plastic sleeves on her arms and legs, presumably to protect her from being knocked against things. Before I prayed for her she told me that she was not able to move at all. "You told me that you believed God was going to heal you," I said after we had prayed for healing. "Now, in Jesus' name, raise your right arm!" Without any sign of pain or discomfort she lifted her arm off the chair. "It's fantastic!" she shouted at the top of her voice. Then she looked at me, as though she could hardly believe what was happening to her; "Can I raise the other one?" she asked. She was also able to raise that arm with ease.

"God has started your healing," I said to the woman. "He will not start something He does not plan to finish. You go to the back of the hall." There were several queues of people waiting for me, at least another hundred people wanting prayer. I had to get on to the next person, so I left the lady to receive the rest of her healing. About half-an-hour later someone came over to me, and pointed to the glass lobby at the back of the hall.

The woman was out of her wheelchair, walking round and round. My wife watched as someone folded up the wheelchair, and the woman walked unaided down the twenty-four steps from the hall to the car park.

Christians are not immune to sickness and disease which come through the work of Satan in the world. But it can be overcome through the healing power in the name of Jesus. In my own life I have learnt to ask God to heal me, and I welcome the prayers of others on my behalf. In the summer of 1985, I was watching television one Sunday afternoon when I felt this sharp pain in my chest. I put my hand on my chest and prayed silently, but the pain got worse and worse, until I did not think I could bear it much more. I did not want to say anything to worry Stella, so I got up and started to walk out of the room. "Where are you going?" my wife asked me. "I am going to make a cup of tea," I replied.

That was the last thing I remember. I came round to find myself on the floor, and the doctor had arrived. When I collapsed on the floor Stella had telephoned him. "I think my husband must be having a heart attack. Come quickly," she said. I was unconscious for nearly half-an-hour. The doctor confirmed that I had indeed had a heart attack, and wanted to take me into hospital at once. I did not want to go to hospital, and in the end he agreed that if I promised not to do anything — scarcely even move a finger for seven days — he would let me stay at home. They got me into bed, and I lay there feeling terrible. I was perspiring heavily, but I felt very cold and most unwell. As soon as the doctor left I turned to Stella. "I must do what I preach. In the Bible we are told to send for the elders of the church to pray for the sick *(James 5:14),* so please will you call Pam Halls (the other elder of our church) and ask her to come over and pray for me and anoint me with oil. We will ask for a new heart." This was done, and I knew that the Lord had healed me.

I stayed in bed for three days and quite enjoyed the rest. On the third day the doctor came and checked how I was, taking my pulse and blood pressure. "You seem to be getting over this attack reasonably well," he said. "We have to wait 48 hours before we can take a blood sample which will tell us how much of the heart has been damaged and how much muscle has died." He took the sample, and said he would come back on the Saturday to see me again. I promised that I would continue to rest, and because I was making good progress the doctor allowed me to sit downstairs by the fire.

The doctor came to see me again a day earlier than I was expecting him. He was smiling broadly when he came into my room. "I could not keep the news to myself any longer; I have got the results of your blood tests, and there is no damage to your heart at all. It is as though you had never had a heart attack." It was marvellous news, but rather what I had expected after our prayers for healing. The doctor gave me a thorough examination and arranged for a follow-up appointment in the future. I felt completely fit and well over the next months, and went off for my appointment, eager to show how well I had recovered.

My own doctor was away at the time and I was seen by a different doctor. He had a good look at my notes, and examined me. "We have changed your notes now to say that you did not have a heart attack," he told me. "Why was that?" I asked. "Well there was no damage to your heart, so it could not have been a heart attack." At the time the doctor had been quite convinced that it had been a heart attack — and I believe it was. When we prayed God had so completely healed me that

94

now this other doctor could not find evidence. The important thing was that I was fit and well again, without any lingering questions about my health.

A few years ago I had a serious accident and cut my nose very severely. There was blood everywhere, and I was rushed straight into hospital where my face was covered in stitches and layers of gauze to stop the bleeding. It was a terrible sight — even after the medical staff had done their best. I was warned that the stitches would have to stay in for several weeks, and then I would probably need plastic surgery. I was in a real quandry. It was only a few days before I was due to take a series of healing services in a church on the south coast. How could I go and tell all these people that God heals today when I looked such a mess, with my face covered with medical dressings? It was not going to encourage anyone's faith!

I have realised over the years how important it is for people to have faith that God is going to heal them. When we respond to God in faith it releases His power to work in our lives. That is why I spend so much time telling stories about people whom God has healed. I have a simple faith in God and in the promises in the Bible. I know that each time we see someone healed, or we hear of something miraculous happening we start to believe that God will also do it in our situation. "The prayer made in faith will heal the sick person; the Lord will restore him to health, and the sins he has committed will be forgiven" *(James 5:15)*. I wanted to encourage faith, and the way I looked with most of my face covered up was not the image most likely to encourage others to listen to what I had to say. "Lord, you know that I have these healing services at the end of the week, and you know what a mess I look at the moment." I prayed that God would touch my face, and speed up the healing process.

The next day I went back to the hospital. The sister in charge of casualty recognised me at once. "What are you doing back here?" she asked. "I have come to have the stitches taken out," I replied. "I told you that they would not come out for ten days." I guess she thought I was a stubborn and probably stupid old man. Eventually I persuaded her to look at my face. When she took all the gauze and dressing off my face was perfectly clear. The swelling round the nose had disappeared, the discolouring of the skin had faded, but most dramatically, the deep cut on my nose had completely healed. The only sign that anything had been wrong was the surgical stitches running down one side of my nose, and across to the other side. It was a great story to tell at the services that weekend. The nurse never could explain what had happened — as far as she was concerned it was quite impossible.

This concept of faith is central to my experience of the healing ministry. Matthew's gospel tells the story of Jesus healing two blind men *(Matthew 9:27ff)*:

'The two blind men came to him, and he (Jesus) asked them, "Do you believe that I can heal you?"

"Yes, sir!" they answered.

Then Jesus touched their eyes and said, "Let it happen then, just as you believe!" — and their sight was restored'. Ever since I first became a Christian I have seen people healed — through Ken Matthew's prayers, through my prayers and those of many other people. Whoever prays, it is Jesus who heals, and it is important to understand healing today in relation to Jesus' healing ministry when he was on earth. He set down certain principles which I think it is important to follow. In the New Testament we see Jesus' compassion for people who are sick, his desire to heal (even when all

96

the sick in the village are brought to him), the way he rebukes Satan's influence which brings sickness to people. I believe that Jesus is the same today, and he is at work in the world through his Holy Spirit in the same way. In the Bible we are encouraged to pray for one another for healing *(James 5:16),* and we should expect to see Jesus continuing his healing ministry through us today.

At the beginning of the ministry on earth Jesus read out a prophecy from the Old Testament in his local synagogue!

> ''The Spirit of the Lord is upon me,
> because he has anointed me to preach good
>   news to the poor.
> He has sent me to proclaim release to the
>   captives
> and recovery of sight to the blind,
> to set at liberty those who are oppressed,
> to proclaim the acceptable year of the
>   Lord.''

When he had read it out Jesus announced that he was the fulfillment of the scripture. This prophecy, right at the beginning of his ministry on earth, is for me a summary or definition of what Jesus came to do. His teaching, preaching, miracles, healings, and eventually his death on the Cross are all a part of this prophecy. As Christians today we see God continuing this work — and in his grace he uses us as His instruments.

8

"Good News to the Poor"

My first and foremost desire is for people to come to know Christ, and for me, spiritual health and salvation is more important than physical healing. Whenever I am asked to minister at a healing service I always want to talk about Jesus' ministry in every part of our lives, not just healing. The New Testament stories about Jesus and his disciples so often show how a miracle or healing made people want to know more about God. I believe that, as with all Christians, I am sent to preach the good news of salvation through Jesus, and I am excited when my preaching and healing ministry come together to bring people to God.

Over the years I have been invited to speak at a number of Full Gospel Businessmen's dinners. These are always interesting evenings, when local businessmen come along with their Christian friends, and a speaker is asked to give his testimony. When I am invited to speak at one of these dinners I tell the story of how I became a Christian, and then I go on to talk about God's healing ministry. Then at the end I offer to pray for people for healing, and I have seen many people healed on these evenings. On one occasion I was asked to speak at a dinner in the Maidenhead area, and I told them stories of some of the miracles I have seen. The following Sunday when I went to church there were three businessmen waiting outside. "We heard you speak at the dinner at Maidenhead, and we have come tonight to see some of the miraculous healings you were talking about," they told me. "It is all very well to say that you have come to see miracles," I told them, "but I do not know if God will do anything miraculous tonight. It is not a show — and there may not be anyone here who is sick and in need of healing." I welcomed them to the service, although I did feel as though they thought I was some sort of theatrical turn.

At the end of the service I asked as normal if there was anyone present wanting prayer for healing. A lady got up out of her seat and walked slowly and stiffly up to where I was standing at the front. Her legs were covered with heavy bandages. She told me that her knee caps had been removed, so that her legs were stiff and she was in terrible pain. I prayed for her and then moved on to pray for someone else while she went away. I am not quite sure what happened next, but I know she went to the back of the church and my wife helped her to take off her bandages. The next thing I knew was that this woman was running up the centre of the church holding her bandages out behind her like streamers. She was skipping and dancing like a lamb and she was able to bend and stretch her knees. Her words bubbled over in her excitement and she told everyone who would listen that the pain had gone and that she could now move freely again.

I took her over to where the three businessmen were sitting. "You said you wanted to see a miracle," I said to them, "and now you have seen one." I left them to talk to the woman, and I could hear them asking all sorts of questions about what had been wrong with her and exactly what had happened now. Sometime later one of the men came up to speak to me. "I have seen a miracle now, but I still cannot believe it — it is impossible." I challenged gently, "Do you think I made it up, or the woman made her story up?" Although he admitted that he did not think that I had in some way 'set it up', or persuaded the woman to pretend for the benefit of other people, he could not accept that God does heal in such ways. His two friends had seen the same thing, and they did believe.

When I went to speak at a Full Gospel Businessmen's dinner in Norwich a young girl came up to me for prayer. She was thirteen years old, but she was so badly crippled with arthritis with thin little arms and legs that she looked about the size of a normal eight or nine year old. Her parents were not Christians but she had come along that evening at the invitation of their next-door neighbour, who was the chairman of the local Full Gospel Businessmen's chapter. As I prayed for the child and watched her go away I felt moved almost to tears. Without God's healing in her life what kind of future would there be for her?

The meeting went on until late at night and I was invited to stay the night at the home of one of the men who had organised the dinner. While we were eating breakfast the next morning the doorbell rang and the chairman burst into the room. "I wanted to catch you before you set off for home," he said. "While I was shaving this morning I looked out of the bathroom window over the front garden. Coming through the gate, running and skipping between her parents, was the little girl from next door for whom you prayed last night.

I did not bother even to finish shaving, but ran downstairs to meet them. The little girl is completely well, and her parents are beside themselves with joy." We talked for a while and then the man left. He had to get home to tell his neighbours more about the God who had so wonderfully healed their child.

After another Full Gospel meeting in Swansea I was asked to visit one Christian woman at her home. "She used to teach in the Sunday-school at church," I was told, "but now she is crippled with multiple sclerosis and she could not manage to get to the meeting tonight." When we arrived at her house the next morning her husband opened the front door to us. He was a big man, who looked as though he should have played rugby for Wales. I knew he was the manager of the local coal mine, and although his wife was a Christian he would not have anything to do with God or church.

I went into the sitting room with the friend who had brought me. There, sitting on the sofa, with a rug over her knees and her hands folded in her lap, was a fragile-looking woman. The wheelchair tucked nearly out of sight behind the sofa was a constant reminder of her sickness. I started to ask questions, to discover the extent of her disability. The woman told me that until two weeks previously she had been able to feed herself, but now she could not even move her hands. She was completely helpless.

Her husband sat on a chair next to the sofa, with his hands on his knees, and I knew he was listening intently to everything I said. I started to talk about God's power to heal, and I asked the woman if she believed that God could heal her. "That is all you need; your faith and God's power — when they meet you get your miracle!" Then I knelt before her and rebuked the spirit of infirmity that had manifested itself in the form of multiple sclerosis, and commanded it to leave her body at once. "Now give me your hands," I said as I held out my hands to her. A few minutes previously she had told me that she could not move her hands, but now she lifted her arms and gripped my hands tightly in her own.

"In the name of Jesus, take off that rug and walk — for the glory of God!" She stood up and moved first one foot and then the other. After her first few hesitant steps she could move freely. There were tears streaming down her face — she could walk again. Her husband jumped up and picked her up as though she was a doll. He hugged her and kissed her, and then gently putting her down he came over and flung his arms around me. "Thank you for healing my wife, thank you, thank you!" "I have not healed her," I tried to explain. "It is this Jesus who you do not believe in — he is the one who healed her." "I do believe now," he said. "Look at my wife walking — I do believe!" We talked further and there and then he accepted Jesus as his Saviour.

My wife had been waiting for me outside in the car, since we had not wanted to crowd too many people into the little home. "I am sorry I kept you waiting so long," I apologised as I got into the car beside her. "You were only about twenty minutes — not long at all," she told me. I looked back at the house, and saw the couple standing by the gate waving after us as we drove away, the wife healed and the husband had become a Christian; it had been a good use of twenty minutes.

I was sitting at home in Abingdon one afternoon when the telephone rang. "Is that Fred Smith?" the lady on the other end asked. "I have heard that God uses you in the healing ministry and I wondered whether you would pray for me?" She told me that she suffered from an advanced case of multiple sclerosis and that she believed God could heal her. "My husband has lifted me out of my wheel chair and propped me on some cushions so that I can reach the telephone while he goes back to work for the afternoon." she explained. "Is it all right to pray over the telephone?"

Since God is everywhere through his Holy Spirit I certainly do not need to be with someone to pray for them. We talked for a few minutes and then I prayed for her. "You told me a minute ago that you believed you would be healed," I reminded her, "Put the telephone down and walk up your hall, then come back and talk to me again." There was a click as though the phone had been put down on the stairs, and then a long period of silence. "Hello, hello, are you still there?" I asked. There was no reply. I was worried that the lady might have fallen and be unable to reach the telephone. I felt rather irresponsible — I had not even asked for her name or address so I did not know who she was or how I could get help to her. All I could do was pray for her.

"Are you still there, Fred?" The question came after what seemed an interminable wait. "I am sorry! I forgot all about you," she said. "After we prayed I tried to move my legs, and then I found I could get up. So I dropped the telephone and walked down the hall. It was marvellous. I went out into the garden and called to my neighbour over the fence, and she could not believe her eyes. I was skipping around like a child, and I started to tell her what had happened. 'This man prayed for me, and now I can walk' I told her. 'What man?' she asked, and I suddenly remembered that you were still at the other end of the telephone. I am sorry to have gone off like that."

What could I say to that? I only wished I was there

to see her walking again. In her excitement she still forgot to give me her name or telephone number, but I will not forget to ask the next person. People often ask whether 'it will work' if we pray over the telephone. I remind them that it is God who heals, and the important thing is that He is with them, not me. The same issue will come up at the meeting. "I do wish my cousin or neighbour could have been here tonight. If only Fred would pray for them I know they would get better." Again and again I have to explain that I am only the channel of God's healing power, and that it is their faith and His power that is important. "My wife is an excellent cook, and she makes beautiful cakes. Supposing she made a cake, and I brought it to you and when you told me how good it was I preened myself, and said 'I do make a good cake don't I?' It would not be true to pretend that I had made the cake myself. It's like that with God: He does the healing and sometimes uses me as the delivery boy.

I asked God to show me some way in which His healing ministry could grow without being limited to me. I can not go to visit all the sick people I hear about, and if I did I would be worried that people would start turning me into some form of guru. Then one day I was sent a 'prayer cloth', with a note explaining that someone had prayed over this cloth, and they believed that God had anointed it as a prayer cloth. In Acts chapter 19 we read of Christians being healed through handkerchiefs and aprons that had been prayed over and taken to them. "God was performing unusual miracles through Paul. Even handkerchiefs and aprons he had used were taken to those who were ill, and their diseases were driven away and the evil spirits would go out of them." If God had worked like that in the past could He not do so again, if we prayed for prayer cloths?

We took small pieces of cloth and prayed over them. We asked God to anoint the cloths with His healing power, and to use them to heal many people. Each prayer cloth was put inside a leaflet explaining about healing through Jesus' name, as well as simple notes on what it means to become a Christian. "As a Christian, place the cloth either on your head, or on the part of the body causing trouble. In the name of Jesus Christ, command the sickness to leave you. Simply believe that God has heard and answered your prayer and receive your healing with a thankful heart. Give Him thanks and praise. Expect miracles and God will honour your faith. You may keep the prayer cloth and use it as often as you like for anyone in need. God's power does not change."

We make the prayer cloths freely available at our church services, and whenever I was asked to speak I would take a pile of envelopes with me, each containing a prayer cloth and leaflet. One of our church members became the Prayer Cloth secretary, and she agreed to send out cloths to everyone who asked. The cloths are completely free, even postage, as none of us want to make any money out of doing God's work. (It is just the same when I go to speak at a meeting.) Since I am now a pensioner I am always grateful when people offer to pay my expenses, but I do not take any payment for myself.) Over a period of three years the Prayer Cloth Secretary sent off over seventeen thousand cloths and in reply we had many letters telling us of marvellous healings.

"Thank you for the prayer cloths you sent. They have gone already and people are waiting for them and passing them on. I do not remember whether I told you of a child being healed of a tumour on the brain? She's at school again now and her hair is growing again. All this has happened since the girl was given up as a hopeless case by doctors all over the world.''

''Please send me four prayer cloths as I have heard of four people who desperately need the healing touch of the Lord Jesus. I know that the Lord works through the prayer cloths because I was given one at the meeting last April and several friends have been healed through it. At the same meeting my husband went forward for healing as he had been suffering from anaemia for several years and was not responding to treatment. Praise God, he was completely healed.''

''I heard of a young girl who suffered from deafness having a prayer cloth on her ear and she could hear about eight hours later. Praise the Lord!''

''Forgive the delay in writing — I wanted to gather as much feedback as possible to keep you informed... The little boy with a squint and a bad heart is now able to do without his glasses (although his eyes are not quite straight yet) and his mother reports his pulse and heart-beat to be quite normal now... The little girl, who was deaf due to meningitis and who the doctor said would not hear again, is now able to hear quite well after the father (who came to the meeting and is a professed atheist) suggested the family pray together over her using a prayer cloth that same evening!... The vicar has not been feeling at all well, but he asked his wife to use the prayer cloth and lay hands on him and has been fine ever since.''

''I write again to ask if you would send me a bigger supply of prayer cloths? ... The healings continue as our Lord never tires or fails... Thank the Lord for the recent healings in his mighty name; angina, unbalanced brain, multiple sclerosis, someone suffering from a cerebral haemorrhage, and for a lady who was an alcoholic and inveterate smoker who has given it up now.''

One lady took a hundred prayer cloths with her when she visited her family in Nigeria. We heard later of every possible kind of healing, including one man raised up healed from his death bed. A Nigerian pastor came to church with her while he was in England to see a top eye specialist because he seemed to be going blind. The day before he returned to Nigeria the specialist told him that there was nothing he could do, and that he would probably go blind. The pastor rang me, we prayed over the telephone and he received his sight.

God has worked in many remarkable ways through the prayer cloths. They are not anything in themselves, but when people use them in faith God often steps in to heal. As a result of the healings many people have become Christians when they have seen God healing them, even without someone praying for them. So often we think that we must pray or preach for people to be healed and converted. Prayer cloths have shown me how God graciously uses us sometimes, but He is not limited to working through us.

I heard recently of a lady from Kidderminster who had been lying sick in bed for twelve years. Eventually she ran out of books to read and things to do, and she picked up a Bible and started to read it. By the time she reached Isaiah she had begun to believe. 'By his stripes we are healed' *(Isaiah 53:5)*. ''Well, if it says we **are** healed what am I doing lying here in bed?'' She believed that Jesus died for her and prayed to receive her healing, then got up out of her bed completely well. She believed God's promise in the Bible, and without anyone praying for her, no tapes on healing or prayer cloths she was miraculously healed. Her faith met God's power, and the miracle happened.

9

"Release to the captives"

Cancer, multiple sclerosis, incurable, malignant — these must be some of the most feared words in the English language. They strike fear into the hearts and minds of those who hear them, and we become captive to the hopelessness they evoke. "I can accept God can heal arthritis, or migraines or whatever, but surely even He cannot heal cancer?" people will ask. Jesus said he came to bring release to the captives, and that includes those captive to every disease and fear of disease — however incurable.

In the summer of 1984 I visited a church in Suffolk where I met Ken. He was one of the first people to come up for prayer at the end of the service, a young man but looking quite ill. "What do you want me to pray about for you?" I asked him. "I have several tumours in the lymph nodes in my groin. I have had one operation, but I am still in great pain, and the tumours are multiplying." Later he told his story more fully.

"I was concerned about a loss of four stone in weight, and after a series of tests at the hospital, doctors found tumours in my lymph nodes in my groin which they suspected were malignant...... Three months had passed by and I wasn't feeling any better.

"A friend of mine who I knew was a Christian asked if I would like to go along to Church with him and his family. This I did and on returning home I found myself thinking about what the vicar had said, which was simply that Jesus loved me. For days I could think of nothing else.

"A couple of weeks later I was feeling very ill and started to think of taking the fool's way out.... When it actually came to the moment to take my exit from this earth, I couldn't do it and that was the moment when I asked the Lord Jesus Christ to take over my life as I couldn't do anything else to help myself.

"From that moment I began to feel better until I went into hospital in December 1983 for an operation which removed two of the tumours in my groin. Praise the Lord they were non-malignant. Everybody seemed happy about this except me! I was still in great pain, more and more tests followed, but still the pain and even more tumours. They seemed to be breeding but nobody knew why.

"As time went on I was getting more and more fed up with the pain and even more disillusioned by the tests because nothing was happening. One Saturday in June 1984 my vicar mentioned to me that a Christian with a healing ministry, Fred Smith, was coming to our area. He told me that God had performed miracles through Fred and I should go and see him.

"On the day, together with twelve others from my church, we went along to where Fred was ministering... The little church was packed, there must have been two hundred and fifty people present. We sang and had a time of prayer before going up for healing. It was

8.40pm when Fred called all those who wanted healing ministry to come forward, and I was fourth to go up. "What is your trouble?" Fred asked me. "I am full of cancer; I am twenty-nine years old, and I do not expect to live until I am thirty." I replied. Fred and I spoke for a while about the illness then he prayed for me, for a complete healing.

"I could feel Fred's hand on my head and groin and I heard him say "In the name of Jesus I command this illness to leave this body." The next thing I knew I felt this terrific pain in my groin and I let out a cry as if my whole body had been turned inside out, then I was rendered unconscious, on my back on the floor. It felt as though I was lying there for ages, but my friends say it was only about two or three minutes.

"When I got up and went back to my friends the emotion was too much and I just hugged some one and cried with happiness. During all the emotion I hadn't realised that I couldn't feel any more pain, but when I did and as soon as my friends and I got home an inspection of my body was necessary. On doing this I found no tumours and the scar from the operation was gone. God had healed me completely. All I needed now was a confirmation from the hospital. This I got on 14th August 1984. I was given a clean bill of health and no more tumours."

A couple of months after I prayed for Ken I was being interviewed on the local radio station. Without telling me they had managed to trace Ken, and they interviewed him about his healing on the same programme. I have often wondered how the doctors at the hospital reacted when this man they had operated on arrived for a check-up, and the scar from the operation had completely disappeared.

I am sometimes asked how medical doctors react to

miraculous healings. I always encourage people to return to their doctors for verification of the healing, but for some people like Dinah Hills it was impossible to go back to the specialists. You cannot normally go to a specialist unless referred by your own family doctor. I do not want people to stop taking any prescribed medicine. If a diabetic is healed, for example, the prescribed dose of insulin may start to make him feel unwell. He should then go to the doctor, and be gradually taken off the medication. Stopping taking medication before there is proof of healing would be irresponsible, and continuing to take medicine does not deny our belief that God is healing. I welcome all that the medical profession does for us, and would not in any sense oppose what they do. I am not medically trained, nor am I attempting to diagnose or treat sickness. But God's healing power is not limited by medical diagnosis or expectation.

In Runcorn recently I met a lady doctor who came forward for prayer during a healing service. Margaret said she had started to experience slight symptoms a year previously but she had ignored them until she discovered a lump in her breast a few weeks before I met her. She went to see another doctor who confirmed her own diagnosis of cancer, and arranged an appointment with a specialist two weeks later. She came to the service I was taking before her appointment with the specialist, convinced that unless God healed her she would need surgery. After the cancer was discovered Margaret, a committed Christian, had spent some time looking at the stories in the Bible about Jesus healing people. As a doctor she knew all the implications of what was happening in her body, and as a Christian she came to God for healing.

I prayed for her and said "In the name of Jesus I command this lump to go.'' Margaret later described her feelings during the prayer time: ''As soon as Fred said it, I felt the lump flip out and I fell back. I had this great sense of being set free and the whole of my body was relaxed.'' She experienced some soreness for the next few days, ''but by the end of the week I felt incredibly good.'' Her appointment with the surgeon served to confirm her healing, and he pronounced her totally clear from cancer.

Often I will pray for many people on a particular evening and leave without knowing whether or not some people have been healed. I always enjoy hearing later what God has been doing for people, from letters like this one:

''Looking back we can praise God that Ben had to have an operation for aneurysm on the groin and a hernia last December, for it was only due to tests and examination at that time that it was revealed that he had a tumour in the lung, which was considered a small one. Ben decided to refuse an operation for the tumour as it was considered exceedingly dangerous due to breathing difficulties. He agreed to have a course of radiotherapy, though he was told that it was not a cure. He was told he would have one year, or at the most two years, to live. It was about three weeks after the end of the course of radiotherapy when you prayed for Ben at the end of March. Ben's chest was X-rayed in April and again in July and the tumour was not to be found. Then they did a deep chest scan (looking inside by a light on wires) and this brought the good news — no tumour! The consultant was very pleased and somewhat surprised but he knew from the start that we were looking to the Lord for healing, whilst accepting whatever medical science could do.''

Whatever the sickness we can be trapped by the seeming hopelessness of the situation. Christine wrote to me a long letter telling me her story after she was healed. "I was born with a slight deformity of the hips which in no way impeded my life as a healthy active schoolgirl until it prevented me taking up a ballet scholarship at the age of eleven. I was told then, that due to this deformity I would never be able to dance. I ignored this and continued to dance and eventually took up teaching ballet. At the age of nineteen (whilst still a student teacher) I was working hard in class and also teaching regularly, when suddenly without warning both my knee caps slipped out of place.

"I went to my doctor, who sent me to the Nuffield Hospital in Oxford. There followed two years of frequent visits, X-rays and physiotherapy, none of which did much good. My knees, for no accountable reason, would quickly swell and I was often in continuous pain. This was the case on the night of 18th September 1974 when I went forward for prayer for healing. My term had started two days earlier, and I had been on my feet non-stop. When I arrived at the meeting straight from work not only my knees but also my ankles were swollen (so much so that the straps of my shoes had been completely covered and were very painful).

"I went to Fred along with others at the end of the meeting, told him briefly about my trouble and he laid hands on me. Suddenly I sat down and began to cry, not realising that I was healed. I was too ashamed of my tears to look up so I studied the floor, and it was then that I noticed what had happened. I could see my shoe straps (the swelling in the ankles had gone down), my knees were no longer swollen and above all there was no pain. I went home rejoicing.

"When I got up the next morning and clambered out of bed I found my knees were hurting. I looked at them

— there was no swelling but the pain was back. I smacked my knees; "Get out Satan — I have been healed in the name of Jesus!" The pain went away at once and I have had no more trouble since, despite continuing to teach ballet.

"I was nineteen when my knees first slipped out of place (due to my hip deformity) and nearly twenty-four when I was healed. The consultant at the Nuffield had told me that it was something 'you will just have live with' as an operation could not guarantee a better state of affairs. I hope this shows how wonderfully the Lord helps our personal needs, both physically and spiritually."

When I visited Cheshire in 1985 a lady came up to me at the end of the meeting, and said "I think I have been healed while you were speaking, even without you praying for me." I asked her what was wrong with her and she told me that for twenty-three years she had suffered from degenerative sclerosis of the spine, which affected the discs and nerves in her spine. She was on medication all the time and suffered considerable pain despite trying epidurals, acupuncture and every possible type of drug to ease the pain. When I met her she was taking forty-eight pain-killing tablets each day to keep herself going.

The week before my visit Sylvia had experienced a burning heat sensation on her face while praying and she had a vision of bright sunlight around her. On the morning of the service she woke up unable to see clearly because of some swelling round the eyes. "The doctor said it was probably a virus, but that if it had been very hot the previous day he would have thought I had been out in strong sunshine to cause the swelling. By midday my eyes had returned to normal, and I was looking foward to the service in the evening.

"At 6.00pm I was eagerly waiting for the service to begin, but I was in terrible pain from my spine. I felt so ill I probably should have left, but I was determined to stay for the service no matter what happened. When the service started I had to sit down as my spine felt as though it was on fire, and this lasted for almost an hour. Then I was able to stand up and the pain had gone."

It seemed that God had indeed healed Sylvia while she was listening to my sermon. I asked if I could pray for her, for God to complete her healing. I laid my hands on her head and asked God to give her a new spine where the discs were pitted with holes. She was filled with the Holy Spirit, "it felt marvellous!" Sylvia did not need to take any medication from then on, and her husband could not believe the difference. He 'complained' about his newly rejuvenated wife. When Sylvia saw her doctor he was very pleased. She was registered as disabled, but will have to wait for three years before she can see the specialist for a check-up. During those three years she will continue to receive a disability allowance from the state, even though she says she has been completely healed.

I have known of other occasions when someone was healed during a meeting. There was a first floor gallery in the hall where the meeting was held, and since the hall was full there were people sitting in the gallery as well. "When Fred invited people to go forward for prayer it felt as though every single person was trying to get out of the gallery and down the steps. The reason I wanted prayer was for a problem with my leg and I did not find it easy to move. When I saw the crowd I would have to get through to get downstairs my heart sank. At that moment Fred looked straight up at the gallery and said, "Don't worry if you cannot get down here — God will heal you wherever you are!'' I felt great heat in my leg, and I was healed where I stood.'' God is longing to heal us, whatever the problem and wherever we are, even if we are trapped in the middle of a sea of people, He will be there with us.

10

"Recovery of Sight to the Blind"

"One thing I do know, that though I was blind, now I see." *(John 9:25)*. When Jesus healed the man near the temple who was born blind it caused an uproar. The Jews did not believe that he had really been blind, and they questioned both his parents and the man himself. There is nothing we can say to explain how such healings happen, but Jesus is still doing them today.

A man in Manchester sent a tape of a talk I had given on healing to a blind friend of his who lived in Surrey. "Listen to this tape and you will hear that God heals today." The blind man decided to listen to the tape one morning while his wife was out. She put the tape recorder by his chair so that he could feel for the buttons to switch the tape on and off, and then she went off shopping.

A couple of hours later on her way home she met her husband walking towards the shops to meet her. As he listened to the stories on the tape he had started to believe that it was possible for God to heal him.

"Lord, I believe you healed all these people, will you heal me now?" he prayed. His sight was fully restored as he listened to the tape.

After a visit to Exeter I was asked by some business-men to hold some services for the holiday makers at Teignmouth. They could not get a hall, so we held the services in the cinema down on the sea front. It was not the easiest place for a service, as I had to stand in front of the screen, and we had to fix up spot lights on either side since the house lights were timed to fade and come up again according to the normal cinema pat-tern. Despite these minor technical problems we had two marvellous services. When I had been home for a few days someone rang me up and told me about a blind man who had been at the service.

The blind man was in the centre of town a couple of days after the service, where he was greeted by an atheist friend. "So you did not go to that healing service in the cinema," said the friend, noticing his white stick and obviously blind eyes. "I did actually, but I can tell you, I do not go much on that Fred Smith," retorted the blind man. "Being blind I have to go by what I can hear, and I heard him saying 'In the name of Jesus get out of your wheelchair, in the name of Jesus do this, in the name of Jesus do that,' to all the people around me. When they put me in front of him all he did was put one hand on my head and said 'God's word is true! Now go and be healed.' He did not say 'In the name of Jesus' or anything."

Then he turned to his friend. "Do you know if there is a book in the Bible called Malachi?" he asked. "I do not know anything much about the Bible, but why do you want to know?" "Ever since Fred put his hand on my head and said 'God's word is true!' I have heard this voice inside my head saying 'Malachi 1,5.' I reckon it must be something to do with the Bible because Fred said 'God's word...' So the blind man sat and waited in the sea-front car park while his friend went off and found a Bible for him. He came back and the blind man asked him to look up the list of books in the front. He found the page number for Malachi, and looked up chapter one, verse five. "Read it out," instructed the blind man. "And your eyes shall see this, and you will glorify the Lord outside the borders of Israel."

As his friend read out the verse the blind man started to see. He could see the cars and the people along the sea-front. "Give me that Bible," he said, and he read out the verse for himself. "Now I know what Fred meant about God's word being true. I can see to read this verse with my own eyes, and I do glorify the Lord!"

On another occasion I prayed for a blind man to receive his sight, and as I prayed I remember saying, "and you will receive your sight in ten days." It seemed a strange thing to say — certainly not something I had thought with my natural mind, but I believe it was the prompting of the Holy Spirit. There were no signs that anything had happened to the man, and he went home a little despondent, and wondering what the next ten days would bring.

There was no sign of any progress or gradual healing over the ten days. Perhaps nothing would happen at all. The man began to wonder if he had dreamt my comment, or whether it was all a con-trick. People kept warning him not to hope too much, but he replied: "That man said ten days, so I am going to give it ten days before I stop hoping." On the morning of the tenth day he woke up, and opened his eyes. The first thing he saw was an old alarm clock sitting by his bedside, and he could read the hands pointing to twenty minutes to eight. "I used to keep that clock beside my bed when

I was blind because it had a loud ticking sound, and it seemed like an old companion," he explained. Now the clock is fully back in use for telling the time. His eyesight was perfectly restored.

I do not know why God chooses to heal different people in different ways and in different times. As soon as I start to think that I understand something about praying for the sick, and how God ministers to people with different diseases I find that God will do something quite extraordinary — like healing someone on the tenth day after prayer.

The newspapers sometimes report how hard it is for people to prove they should be classified as disabled. Sometimes it is even harder to prove they should be de-classified. A blind lady in Bournemouth came forward for prayer one evening, and as soon as I prayed for her she received her sight. Many people knew her, and there was great excitement at her healing. She made an appointment at the eye hospital so that her name could be taken off the blind register. But when she saw the doctors they refused to accept that she could see. Parts of her eyes did not work, and medically it was impossible for her to see. Any sight she had would undoubtedly deteriorate quickly — perhaps a bump on the head had given temporary sight, but it would not last. "Come back in three months, and we will check again," the doctor said.

The lady knew that she could now see, and that she had not been able to see before we prayed. If the doctor would not take her name off the register it did not really matter — it was rather frustrating but it did not penalize her in any way. She decided to carry on with her life and enjoy the benefits of what she could do now that she could see. This included learning to drive for the first time. Three months later when she went for her next appointment she was sent away from the hospital again. "Even if you can see now it may not last for long. Come back again in three months."

During the next three months she continued her driving lessons, took her driving test and passed. She bought a car, and when it was time for her next appointment she drove herself to the hospital and parked in the car park. The doctors finally decided to take her name off the blind register. "We cannot explain what has happened, but we accept that you can see, and that your sight has now lasted for several months." She invited the doctors to walk out to the car park with her, where she showed them her car and told them how she had learnt to drive and passed her driving test — including of course the eye-sight test — and had been driving around Bournemouth for six months while registered blind. Sometimes our rules and regulations are not flexible enough to cope with what God does.

On two nights running, in different parts of the country I met two young girls with remarkable faith. Both came up for prayer wearing very thick glasses with corrective lenses, which suggested severe short-sightedness. The first girl came up to me, and took off her glasses, asking me to pray for her eyesight to be fully restored. "I can hardly see more than a few yards in front of me without my glasses," she said, "but I am convinced that God is going to heal me tonight." With that she threw her glasses on the ground and stamped on them to smash them. Her faith was such that I hardly had to pray before her eyesight was dramatically improved, and she was able to read small print easily without any aid. Someone said rather cynically later that he suspected that she probably had a spare pair of glasses in her handbag. I did not agree. The girl's dramatic gesture in smashing her glasses was matched by the earnest and trusting expression in her face when she told me that she believed she was going to be healed. As far as she was concerned smashing her glasses was a sign of her faith that God was indeed going to heal her. No one had done that before when I prayed, and to my astonishment the same thing happened on the following evening. I was in a different part of the country (it had taken me most of the day to travel between the two towns) and I had not mentioned the story of the girl from the previous evening to anyone. The second girl also noticed a dramatic improvement in her sight.

On another occasion another woman came for prayer. She was also wearing thick lenses in her glasses, and told me that she had very bad sight. She believed that God was going to heal her, and so we prayed for her sight to be completely restored. When I finished praying the woman opened her eyes and then burst into tears. "It is even worse than before," she cried. "Everything is blurred!" She took off her glasses to wipe the tears from her eyes, and it was then that she realised that she had indeed been healed. Her sight was now perfect, and the thick lenses of her glasses had distorted her vision making everything seem blurred and out of focus. As soon as she took off her glasses everything was clear again.

Watching people as their eyes focus, perhaps for the first time, or with new strength and power is one of the most exciting and dramatic results of prayer. Many of them can hardly believe it for themselves. "One thing I do know: I was blind and now I can see." *(John 9:25)*.

11

"To Set at Liberty Those Who Are Oppressed"

All sickness, in whatever form, be it depression or cancer, comes from the devil. I mentioned earlier (chapter seven) the story in the Bible of a woman bent double for eighteen years, who could not stand up straight, until Jesus laid hands on her and healed her. The Jews in the synagogue were angry that this should have happened on the Sabbath, and Jesus' response to them is very informative.

"Ought not this woman, a daughter of Abraham who Satan has bound for eighteen years, be loosed from this bond on the sabbath day?" *(Luke 13:16)*.

Jesus identifies the author of bondage to sickness when he says "whom Satan has bound." In *(Acts 10:38)* Peter, preaching about Jesus, tells "how he went about doing good and healing all who were oppressed by the devil." This also indicates that sickness is caused by oppression from the devil — you only need to be healed if you are sick.

The devil does not undertake to visit each one of us. He may attack some of the mighty men of God, as he tempted Jesus in the wilderness, but normally he uses his agents for this work. The Bible calls them demons or evil spirits. The two terms are interchangeable; in *Mark 7:25* we read of a woman whose daughter had 'an unclean spirit', yet referring to the same incident in *Matthew 15:22* the woman said her daughter was 'demon-possessed.' We may be attacked by one or more of Satan's hordes of demons.

There is much confusion and fear caused by the use of the phrase "being possessed by an evil spirit." To be possessed means to be under total ownership and absolute control. I possess my car; it is under my absolute control and ownership, it is mine to do with whatever I like. I can take a mallet and smash it about if I want to, because it is mine, and no-one else has any right to say how I should treat it (except perhaps my wife!). Very few people are entirely possessed by an evil spirit or demon. The Greek word, which has been translated as 'possessed' in the Bible actually means 'being under the influence of' or 'in some way being affected by' demons.

Before I became a Christian I used to smoke twenty cigarettes a day. Although the health hazard was unknown in those days, we had a growing family and I could not really afford to smoke and so I tried again and again to give up smoking, but without success. In the end I had to take a part-time job to pay for my tobacco habit. Even when I became a Christian I could not kick the habit, which shows that there was an area of my life still influenced by a demon. When I had become a Christian I had been lifted out of Satan's kingdom into the kingdom of the Son of God by the Holy Spirit. We are not at that time necessarily filled by the Holy Spirit or possessed by the Holy Spirit. We have only just started on our walk with the Lord, and there are many areas of our lives which are not surrendered to him, upon which demons can have an influence.

When I was filled with the Holy Spirit all desire to smoke immediately left me. I had no withdrawal symptoms or cravings for a cigarette at all. This proved to me without any doubt that the Holy Spirit does not like us to smoke. He needs a clean temple to dwell in, and as he came in to my life the demon of nicotine had to leave me.

This blissful state lasted for five years. By this time I was travelling long distances every day, and I found myself remembering how comforting I had found my pipe when I was driving. It was like an old companion. I was being tempted, and I gave in easily. "I can just suck the pipe; there's no need to smoke anything," I told myself. So I went out and bought a pipe, and it was only a short while before I bought some tobacco to smoke. As soon as I realised I was smoking again I tried to stop, but I could not give it up.

No one smoked at the church to which I belonged. I did not want anyone to discover my secret habit, partly because I was so embarrassed that the smoking seemed to control me. I did not want anyone to hear the matches jingling around in my pocket, so I went out and bought a cigarette lighter. That gave access to a little demon of deceit into my life, and I was trapped again. One day someone must have noticed the smell of stale tobacco — although I tried to hide it, sucking strong mints to disguise the smell. "Do you smoke, Fred?" he asked. "Not me!" I lied, and gave access to another demon. Satan is so subtle, and his demons are ready to come into our lives as soon as we give them access. I was not possessed by demons, but that area of my life was definitely influenced by them and outside of my control.

You cannot defeat demons on your own. They are very well organised. Like wild dogs they keep building up their strength until they pull down their victim by sheer weight of numbers. To the demons of nicotine and deceit in my life were added demons of guilt, misery and shame, because by this time I was going out ministering for the Lord. Mercifully the Lord heard my cries and I was delivered from their control. Once the demons had found an area of my life that they could take over, it was as though that part of my life belonged to Satan. They could have been spirits of infirmity or cancer or anything that would have worked out their purpose in my body.

Demons are earthbound and their greatest desire is to have an earthly body to operate in. If it is a blaspheming demon it needs a body to blaspheme through, or a demon of lust needs a body to operate lust through. In Mark 5:10 when Jesus met the man known as Legion the demoniac, the demons entreated Jesus not to send them out of the man. They asked if they could enter the swine rather than be without a body. Demons have awareness and even specific knowledge; when Jesus was teaching in the synagogue *(Mark 1:12-16)* a man with a demon cried out "What have you to do with us, Jesus of Nazareth? Have you come to destroy us? I know who you are, the Holy One of God." In Acts 19 the seven sons of Sceva, a Jewish priest, were trying to cast out evil spirits, when one spirit cried out, "Jesus I know and Paul I know; but who are you?" (verse 15). The man with the demon leapt on them and attacked them.

About twenty years ago I was asked to minister to a young girl who was suffering from deep depression.

When I entered the room she started to speak in a very deep voice, and I recognised that this was a demon speaking through her, rather than the girl herself. "I know you Fred, but you are not strong enough to fight me." "I know you too, and I am not afraid of you," I replied. "Neither do I intend to fight you in my own strength, but with the power in the name of Jesus, the Son of God." I was immediately kicked in the stomach by this girl who was half-demented. A little time later she was set free from the evil spirit by the power in the name of Jesus.

Demons also have the ability to speak. I once had a long conversation with an evil spirit when I went to see a young woman who had attempted to commit suicide. When I met the woman I discerned through the power of the Holy Spirit guiding me that the girl was afflicted by an evil spirit who had caused her to attempt suicide. The spirit started to talk to me, and told me that it was a familiar spirit, that it had been in both the girl's mother and grandmother, and had caused both of them to commit suicide. When I commanded this thing to leave her in the name of Jesus she was set free. Sometimes spirits will be quite violent when they are forced out, and just as Jesus did, we have to command them to come out quietly.

A demon's main activities are to torture, enslave, and drive a person to compulsion. People can be compulsive eaters, or compulsively not eating with anorexia, compulsively smoking or swearing, or drinking. They fight against your peace in every way so that you can never really relax. They spoil relationships in a thousand ways, and their aim is to see the unsaved permanently tortured after death.

A Christian's life is like a hotel with a hundred rooms. The Holy Spirit may occupy even ninety rooms, but there still may be ten rooms occupied by things left from our old pre-Christian nature, fear, resentment, greed, anger, jealousy, unforgiveness. A situation may arise where for an understandable reason we are tempted to sin. Perhaps someone does something that wrongs us, and we feel resentful. We need to deal with this hurt and resentment at once, and ask God to bring healing through his Holy Spirit. Ask a Christian friend to pray for you, and invite the Holy Spirit to take away the hurt and resentment, and help you to forgive the person concerned.

If we allow any hurt or resentment to take a foothold in our lives it can quickly dominate us, and may be accompanied by an evil spirit to control us. When we perpetually sin, or allow sin to fester in our lives we are pulling down God's hedge of protection. We are in effect choosing to take parts of our lives outside of His control and Satan's forces are always waiting to come in. Little things can grow to enormous proportions until they destroy us, just like a little seed of jealousy grew into a monster that destroyed Othello in Shakespeare's play.

It is important for Christians to be aware of these evil forces so that we can resist temptation, and not allow any access point for Satan in our lives. "Resist the devil, and he will flee from you." *(James 4:7)*. This important promise is followed by some useful instructions in the Bible:

"Draw near to God and he will draw near to you. Cleanse your hands, you sinners, and purify your hearts you double-minded."

Prevention is better than cure. We need to deal with the things in our lives that make us 'dirty' in God's eyes, bringing the Holy Spirit into each area of our lives.

All sicknesses do not necessarily mean the presence

of an unclean spirit. I have met people who have had their ear drums perforated by a loud noise; their deafness does not indicate the presence of a deaf spirit, for example. When I pray for people I have to depend solely on the Holy Spirit to help me discern when sickness is caused by an afflicting spirit and when it is not.

Sometimes something happens to make it very obvious — like when the young girl kicked me in the stomach with what felt like the force of ten men. I remember standing up at the front of a church on one occasion, and a man came foward and asked me to pray for him. I prayed for relief from asthma and for the man to be freed from his smoking habit. When I commanded the demon of nicotine to leave him, in the name of Jesus, he was free. Although he was not smoking a pipe or cigarette, there were tendrils of smoke curling round his mouth. The curls of smoke were an obvious sign of the demon showing itself. Sometimes a demon will manifest when we mention the name of Jesus — he is the light of the world, and in the presence of his light the forces of darkness have to show themselves.

I remember meeting a young man, who from childhood had been in and out of mental hospitals. He had changed from a normal happy child to one suffering from deep depressions, and was officially registered as manic depressive. Despite all sorts of drugs to stabilise his condition he was still far from well. He had come along to a service, and asked someone if I would pray for him. I suggested we should go somewhere quiet and private to pray, away from anyone watching him, so we went into a small room adjoining the main body of the church. As we walked into the room I said ''I gather you would like me to pray for you,'' and with that he turned and jumped at me, knocking me to the ground. One minute he was walking along normally and the next he was acting like a wild man, with super-human strength.

I realised that this was a demon (or more than one) manifesting and controlling the man. He put up a fierce fight, and I could easily have been badly hurt. The demons were fighting to prevent me commanding them to leave, so that the man could be free. As we struggled on the floor I started to command them to leave, telling them that they had no power or authority because of Jesus' death on the Cross. It took some time, but eventually he stopped trying to strangle me, and lay still. I helped him up onto a chair.

"What has happened to you?" he asked, looking at me in some surprise. "You look as though you have been in a fight." I looked down at my clothes ruefully. I was a real mess, with my suit covered in dust from rolling on the floor and my shirt and tie pulled about. "Who were you fighting?" the man asked. "Don't you remember?" I asked. "I was fighting you!" He was horrified, and I told him that something bad had been controlling his life, but that now he was free because of Jesus. We prayed together and walked back into the hall, the man now definitely in his right mind. I had a letter from his mother some months later. He had shown no further signs of mental illness, and now was employed in his first job. "It is like having my son back again after so many years." said his mother.

I have used this dramatic story to illustrate that we really are fighting a battle against evil forces. It is only through the power of the Holy Spirit that we can defeat these evil spirits, but we do have the victory. We may be fighting a battle, but Jesus won the war through his death.

A young man came forward for prayer one evening

when I was visiting a small prayer group near Witney. "I have never been able to write," he said. "Will you pray for me?" He told me that there was nothing physically wrong with his hands — he was in fact a skilled carpenter — but he had never been able to learn to write. He could not control a pen with his hands. "Have you never worked for a company where you have had to sign your name in receipt of your wages, or something similar?" I asked, wondering how he had survived without being able to write. "I put the pen in one hand and hold it firmly, then I push that hand with the other, and the pen makes a line on the paper, and that has to count as my signature. It is not letters or anything, but it is the best I can do."

I asked him to hold out his hands and I looked at them. He had fine shaped fingers and strong wrists, and there was no sign of any scarring on wasted muscles, or indeed anything that could account for his disability. I asked God to show me how to pray, and as the man turned his hands over I saw a shadow over the knuckles in each hand. I recognised that I was 'seeing' this with my spiritual eyes, and that these shadows were little demons controlling his hands. I prayed and commanded the demons to leave, and saw the shadows lift off his hands. The spirits controlling his hands had prevented him from writing, condemning him to untold misery and embarrassment, and to some extent ruining his life. When I left the meeting he came up to me and pressed a scrap of paper into my hands. "These are the first words I have ever written," he said. On the piece of paper, in well-formed clear writing, was his name and address, which looked as though it had been written by an adult who had been writing for many years. I have kept the paper in my Bible, as a reminder of the fact that when God brings freedom to someone they are free indeed. "Thanks be to God who gives us the victory through our Lord Jesus Christ" *(1 Corinthians 15:57).*

12

"The Acceptable Year of the Lord's Favour"

My hope is that the stories in this book will encourage people to dare to believe that God can heal them, whatever their problem. The stories are only a small selection from the large number of letters I receive or stories I have been told about people who have been healed. I have been involved in praying for the sick for over twenty-five years and I must have prayed for thousands of people. There are many people from whom I have never heard, and I assume that some of them were healed and some were not. I have chosen to tell stories about the ones who were healed, because my aim is to encourage people to believe in healing. That does not mean that everyone is healed — some are healed, some are not healed.

I believe that one of the signs of the Kingdom of God is the end of sickness and suffering. When mankind turned its back on God, the 'fall of man' *(Genesis 3)*, sin and sickness came into the world through Satan who comes to deceive and destroy. When Jesus was born into the world — both God and man — he said, "The Kingdom of God is at hand." The Kingdom of God — God's rule on earth — had burst into the world through the birth of Christ. When Jesus died on the Cross and rose again from the dead he defeated Satan and his forces, and established God's rule on earth.

However, it is not yet obvious that God is ruling over the whole of the earth, and that Satan is still alive and well. The Kingdom of God is both now, and not yet. "Not yet" — God's rule will not be complete until Jesus comes again as Judge and Satan is put under his feet; but also "now" because we already experience some of the blessings and benefits of God's rule in our lives today.

In the area of healing the "now" aspect of the Kingdom of God is evident in part in the healings and miracles that we see. Miracles of new life in Jesus, miracles of physical healing, emotional restoration, and lives put back together. But because the Kingdom of God is also "not yet" we do not see the power of God in all its fullness.

I believe that this "now and not yet" principle explains in some part why not everyone is healed. For some reason God chooses to limit His power and does not always step in to heal. Equally there may be something in our life which blocks our healing, and allows Satan's forces access to our lives. When we come to the Lord for healing we need to come with clean hearts and clear consciences, confessing our sins and receiving the forgiveness that He offers to us. Sin spoils our lives — it destroys our relationships, our minds, our hearts and even our bodies. Healing brings glory to God, and when people are not healed I will search my heart to make sure there is nothing in my life to prevent them receiving healing. Then I can simply trust God to fulfill His purposes. There are times when there is no obvious blockage, and yet God does not heal. I do not understand why this is, but I have to trust that God is sovereign and in control and that He is ultimately victorious — even over the power of death.

I have been asked whether it might not be better for people to accept their sickness rather than live with the hope of healing. It is undoubtedly hard to lose those we love, or to suffer from sickness ourselves, whether or not we have been prayed for, and are hoping in God for healing. I know this from my own experience. Just under a year ago my eldest grandaughter went into hospital for tests. On her 20th birthday we were told that she had leukemia, and that there was no treatment that could really help her. My grandaughter was a deeply believing Christian, and she knew that God had healed many people of that and other forms of cancer. After she was told the diagnosis she turned to her mother, "Ask Grandpa to come here and pray for me. I will be all right." I prayed, and so did many other people. We watched Nicola growing weaker and weaker, but finding deep peace and comfort in her relationship with God. We kept hoping and we kept praying, but eventually she died. It was a devastating loss for all the family. This young girl, at the start of her adult life, died only months before she was due to get married. Yet I still believe, and I know that Nicola also believed Paul's word in Romans chapter 8:

"For I am sure that neither death, not life, nor angels, nor principalities, nor things present, nor things to come, nor powers, nor height, nor depth, nor anything else in all creation, will be able to separate us from the love of God in Christ Jesus our Lord." *(Romans 8:38)*.

My grandaughter's death was, and still is a cause of great sorrow to me. I do not understand why she was not healed. But I do trust in God's supreme victory and sovereignty, and ultimately I can say "I do not understand, but I do believe." Her death has not in any way destroyed my faith in God to heal, nor prevented me from feeling compassion for those who are sick, and wanting to pray for them. Even if only one person was healed as a result of my prayers it would still be worthwhile — one person healed is a lot better than no-one.

I am sure that it is always good to pray for healing, and if we do not see signs of physical healing that does not destroy the value of our prayers. Some time ago I was asked whether after the meeting I would visit a lady suffering from cancer. She lived forty miles away from the place where the meeting was held, but it would not be far out of my route on my way home, so I arranged to stop off the following morning. It was a complicated route, across country and so we went in two cars, with a friend of the woman showing me the way. As we drove up and parked outside the woman's house the local vicar cycled past us on his way back from the village bakery with a loaf of bread in his bicycle basket. He asked if we were going to visit the lady with cancer, and when we explained that we had come to pray for her the vicar asked if he could accompany us. The three of us knocked on the farmhouse door, and were shown upstairs to where the woman lay in bed. She looked pale and frightened as she lay back against her pillows, a sick and frail woman. The cancer appeared to be in the late stages, and medically there was very little hope for her.

I sat down on one side of the bed, and the vicar sat on the other side, while her friend and one or two members of the family gathered round the bed. I started to talk to the woman about the wonderful works of Jesus, and I told her some stories about people who had been healed. The friend who had brought me to the house was able to tell some stories about people who had been healed only the previous evening. When I sensed that the lady was more relaxed and feeling encouraged by the stories she had heard I suggested that we should pray together.

There was no sign of dramatic healing that morning. As I left the house the vicar told me how glad he was to have been involved. "I am glad we ran out of bread and I was sent to the bakery first thing. I do not know what your prayers have done for this woman, but hearing those stories, and being here to pray has done wonders for my faith." As for the woman, I am convinced that our prayers for her brought some benefit. When I said goodbye to her and left the room I noticed that there was a new sense of calm and serenity about her. Still frail-looking, she seemed no longer fearful of the future, rather hopeful for whatever it might bring.

When we pray for someone it has several effects. The very fact that we are concerned to pray shows that we care, and it is always beneficial to realise that people care. Secondly, when we pray we are asking God's blessing on that person, and together we enter into the presence of God. Thirdly, there is the possiblity and opportunity for healing. At the very least I believe that God blesses every person for whom I pray.

Two weeks ago I prayed for a young man who was a haemophiliac. Suffering since birth from this terrible disease he is used to bleeding internally once a week on average. He was wearing support bandages on his elbows, knees and ankles. I prayed for him one evening and he took away a prayer cloth to encourage him to continue to pray for complete healing. When I saw him ten days later he came up to me smiling all over his face. He had not had any bleeding in the period since I had first met him. Although he was still experiencing some discomfort he attributed this to the arthritic condition resulting from years as a haemophiliac rather than to the disease itself. He told me that he had been able to leave off all the support bandages except one on his ankle, and instead he was praying every night, placing the prayer cloth on each affected place in turn. He promised to let me know any news after his next routine hospital check-up. "It is too early to say that I have been healed, but I definitely feel better," he told me.

In the Old Testament book of Numbers, God tells His people that he will give them the land of Canaan, their Promised Land. They sent one man from each of the twelve tribes to spy out the land, and they came back laden down with good things; a single cluster of grapes was so large that two men carried it together. "It is a land flowing with milk and honey." they said, "but the people are like giants." Although God had promised to give them the land, and despite all the good things they had seen, the people of Israel were too frightened to go in and fight for the land. Only two of the spies encouraged them to enter the land; Joshua and Caleb reminded the people of God's promise: "If the Lord delights in us, he will bring us to this land and give it to us, a land which flows with milk and honey" *(Numbers 14:8).* Because the people were too afraid of the giants to enter the land they spent a further forty years wondering around the wilderness before they entered the Promised Land.

I sometimes think that there are things in our lives today that seem like giants. There are giants of cancer, depression, blindness, deafness; giants of intellect, doubt, fear and unbelief. Does our particular giant frighten us away from entering in to the promised land of all that Jesus has won for us on the Cross? Our promised land is salvation and eternal life with God, and some of the fruit from that promised land may be healing and deliverance. In the healing ministry I feel rather like a travel agent. The travel agent makes all the arrangements for a wonderful holiday, and helps solve some of the difficulties, but he does not pay for the holiday. When I pray for people it can be rather like that; I can help them face their particular giant, and accept the healing for which Jesus has already paid on the cross. It is my prayer that no one should miss out of the promised land because of fear of giants. The giants have already been defeated at Calvary.

For Further Reading

Power Evangelism
   John Wimber (Hodder and Stoughton)

Hidden Warfare
   David Watson (Send the Light)

Fear No Evil
   David Watson (Hodder and Stoughton)

Christian, Set Yourself Free
   Graham Powell (New Wine Press)

Heaven Here I come
   Jean Darnell (Lakeland)

I Believe in Miracles
   Katherine Kuhlman (Lakeland)

Risen with healing in His wings
   Peter Scothern (New Wine Press)

Alive Again
   Bill Banks (New Wine Press)

How to heal the sick
   Stuart Gramenz (Sovereign World)